CAMBRIDGE TRAVEL BOOKS

THE
EARLIEST VOYAGES ROUND
THE WORLD, 1519—1617

No. 9

NOCTURNUM PRÆLIUM
Battalh by night

THE
EARLIEST VOYAGES
ROUND THE WORLD
1519–1617

EDITED BY

PHILIP F. ALEXANDER, M.A.

HERTFORD COLLEGE, OXFORD

Cambridge:

at the University Press

1916

CAMBRIDGE UNIVERSITY PRESS
Cambridge, New York, Melbourne, Madrid, Cape Town,
Singapore, São Paulo, Delhi, Tokyo, Mexico City

Cambridge University Press
The Edinburgh Building, Cambridge CB2 8RU, UK

Published in the United States of America by
Cambridge University Press, New York

www.cambridge.org
Information on this title: www.cambridge.org/9781107600621

First published 1916
First paperback edition 2011

A catalogue record for this publication is available from the British Library

ISBN 978-1-107-60062-1 Paperback

PREFACE

THE aim of the present series is to illustrate the history of geographical discovery by means of select voyages and travels. These are usually written by the discoverer himself, or by an eye-witness who accompanied him on his journey. Apart from the results achieved, they are full of interest, since they tell the story of man's bravery in feeling his way over an unknown world.

The English voyages of the sixteenth century (some of which will be given in this series) record, moreover, the deeds of the seamen who laid the foundation of Britain's sea-power and of her Colonial Empire.

It is hoped that these books may be of service in schools, used either as Readers, or as an aid to the teaching of Geography. Spelling and punctuation have been modernized wherever necessary, though archaic words have been kept.

P. F. A.

WALBERSWICK,
May 1915.

In the hundred years covered by this volume there were six voyages round the world—one Spanish, led by a Portuguese; two English; and three Dutch.

The first of these—that of Magellan—was by far the most noteworthy for its results, and remains probably the most wonderful voyage in the whole history of discovery. Of the rest, Drake's voyage has always had an especial appeal to the imagination of his countrymen, and was a powerful stimulus to English colonization. The last of the six—that of Le Maire and Schouten—is notable for its discovery of Cape Horn and a new passage into the Pacific.

P. F. A.

STEEP,
    April 1916.

CONTENTS

MAPS AND ILLUSTRATIONS

Maps and Illustrations

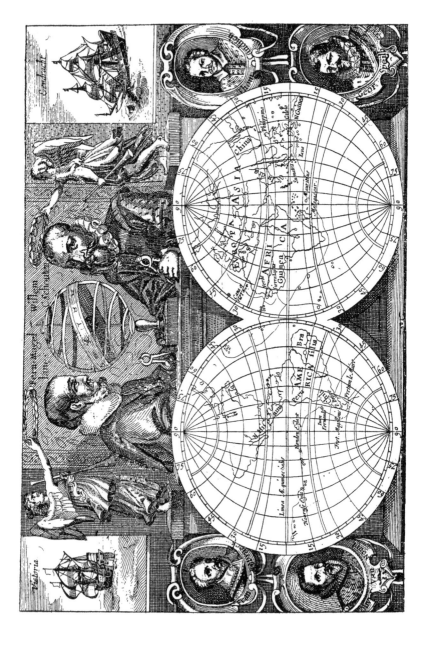

INTRODUCTION

Of the voyages included in this volume, not one was made primarily for the sake of sailing round the world. All were with the object either of discovering a new route to the East, or of commercial gain, or of deliberate plunder—combined in Drake's case with a desire to find lands suitable for colonization.

Of these the voyage of Magellan—by far the most important in its geographical results—was the outcome of the acute rivalry between the two great maritime nations, Spain and Portugal.

At the beginning of the sixteenth century the Portuguese working gradually down the coast of Africa, and past the Cape of Good Hope, had established themselves on the coast of India and in the East Indies; finally in 1521, by their seizure of the Moluccas, or Spice Islands, obtaining the monopoly of the valuable trade with the East.

It was to find another, and as he thought nearer, route to China and India, that Columbus, under Spanish auspices, sailed westwards across the Atlantic in 1492. Owing to his discoveries, Spanish energies were mainly directed towards America, and a series of explorations followed, proving that a vast continent blocked the way between Europe and the East.

The Bull of Pope Alexander VI in 1493, practically dividing the world in two, and giving the western half to Spain and the eastern to Portugal, did not stop the rivalry between the two nations, partly owing to the vague position of the dividing line, and partly because each continued to desire a share of the advantages arising from the other's discoveries.

If the position of this dividing line in the West through the Atlantic was vague, its position in the East, owing to the state of geographical knowledge, was far more uncertain still. Hitherto no European had sailed across the Pacific, and although Balboa had seen it from the Isthmus of Darien in 1513, its great width was still unknown. Moreover it was quite uncertain whether there was any passage connecting the Atlantic and Pacific. There was in fact a widely-held belief that South America expanded in the south into a great continent (the Unknown Southern Land— *Terra Australis Incognita*) that stretched towards the South Pole. The eager desire of the Spaniards for such a passage is shown by the fact that they seriously discussed the possibility of cutting through the Isthmus of Panama, if a strait could not be found.

Magellan (Magalhaes) was a Portuguese nobleman who had already served his country in the East, and assisted in the conquest of Malacca. As his scheme for discovering a new route westwards to the Moluccas met with no support from his own King, he denaturalised himself and turned (like Columbus) to Spain. Here he entered the service of the Emperor, Charles V, and receiving the necessary support, started with five ships under his command in 1519, with the avowed objects of finding the shortest route to the Moluccas, and of proving that they lay within the Spanish sphere.

By January 1520 the expedition had arrived at the

Rio de la Plata (the existence of which was already known), and here a careful search was made for a possible opening westwards. Owing to some months being spent in winter quarters at Port St Julian, they did not arrive at the actual strait (called the Patagonian Strait on Pigafetta's map) until October 21. This strait, some 320 miles long, was traversed in five and a half weeks, the land to the south being named by Magellan Tierra del Fuego (the Land of Fire), owing to the many fires seen there.

The three ships now remaining (one of the original five had been wrecked, and one had deserted) emerged into the South Sea—which they afterwards named the Pacific, owing to the absence of storms—on November 28. Here, although they thought the end of the voyage might be near, their worst sufferings were to begin, and for ninety-eight days they sailed across the ocean, suffering from starvation and scurvy, until they reached the Ladrone Islands on March 6. They next discovered the islands called by Magellan St Lazarus, but in 1542 renamed the Philippines after Philip II. Here, in the island of Mactan, after practically arriving at the goal of his journey, Magellan was killed on April 27, 1521, in a battle between native kings in which he took part.

He had accomplished what is probably the most wonderful voyage in the history of geographical discovery, though he had not found a shorter way to the Moluccas, and though these islands, after much wrangling between Spain and Portugal, remained in the possession of the latter country. After his death the voyage was continued in two ships only, the *Trinidad* and the *Victoria*, the third ship being burnt as unserviceable, after her cargo had been transhipped into the others. They touched at Borneo, and reached the Moluccas early in November. By the middle of December, they were ready to sail homewards laden with spices, when it was found that the *Trinidad* was leaking seriously. The *Victoria* therefore sailed back alone, with Sebastian del Cano as captain, and arrived at Seville on September 8, 1522—the first ship to sail round the world. By far the longest and most detailed account of the voyage is that written by Antonio Pigafetta, an Italian gentleman, who had obtained permission to take part in the expedition and who was one of the few survivors.

The *Trinidad*, after repairing, started on the backward journey for Panama and reached the latitude of 43° N. and about 175° W. longitude, but owing to disease and want of provisions, was obliged to return to the Moluccas, where the crew were seized by the Portuguese, and only four ultimately reached Spain. Whilst the Portuguese were unlading the *Trinidad* at Ternate, she went ashore and broke up in a heavy storm. Her voyage towards Panama was of importance, since it proved the existence of a wide ocean north of the equator, and east of Asia.

For more than fifty years, while conquest and exploration continued in both North and South America, and attempts were made to discover a North-East or North-West Passage, no other ship sailed round the world.

Francis Drake, who had taken part in the third voyage of Hawkins (1567), claimed to have sustained heavy losses owing to the treachery of the Spaniards. In 1573 he had seen the Pacific from the top of a high tree in the isthmus, and had prayed God "to give him life and leave to sail once in an English ship upon that sea." These two events supplied the motives for his voyage of 1577. He set out with a licence from Queen Elizabeth, intending not only to recoup himself for his losses by plundering the Spaniards in the unfortified ports of Peru, but to make an exploration of unoccupied lands, in the hope of finding some suitable for English Colonies. After passing through the Straits of Magellan he was driven by a storm far to the south, and saw islands (one of which he named Elizabeth Island) and possibly Cape Horn—thus to a certain extent disproving the existence of a continent immediately to the south of South America. Sailing up the coasts of Chile and Peru, he loaded his ship with gold and silver and other spoils taken from the Spaniards, and then proceeded to explore part of the coast of California, and took possession of it in the name of the Queen of England, calling the country Nova Albion. On his return, after sailing across the Pacific and Indian Oceans, he was knighted by Queen Elizabeth on the deck of his ship, the *Golden Hind*, and his voyage remains one of the most famous of English voyages. It appealed strongly to the imagination of his countrymen, and was a powerful stimulus to them in their struggle for empire[1].

[1] Very many original Spanish documents still exist, which give minute details of Drake's raid. They consist of reports from officials to King Philip II, depositions of prisoners taken by Drake, etc. These have been translated and edited by Mrs Nuttall in *New Light on Drake* (Hakluyt Society). For the most part, though the evidence of enemies, they give a very favourable impression of Drake, who usually treated his prisoners with much good humour and humanity. It appears that he spoke Spanish fluently, and was a skilled artist who spent much time with his cousin John Drake "shut up...in his

The next voyage round the world, that of Sir Thomas Cavendish (1586–88), was successful in its object of gathering a great store of treasure from the Spaniards. Its main geographical interest was the discovery of King Philip's City, which had been built to defend the Straits of Magellan.

There then followed two Dutch voyages, that of Van Noort (the first Dutch captain who sailed round the world) with Melis—an Englishman who had accompanied Cavendish—as pilot, in 1598–1601, and that of Speilbergen (1614–17). In these there was more fighting and plundering of Spaniards; but valuable knowledge was also obtained.

The sixth voyage of circumnavigation is notable for the discovery of Staten Island and Cape Horn, and a new passage into the Pacific. A charter had been granted to the Dutch East India Company giving them

cabin...painting" new species of "birds, trees and sea-lions." It is to be specially noted that no Spaniard was killed during the capture of ships. A letter from Francisco de Zarate to the Viceroy of Mexico, written a few days after his ship had been captured, is full of interesting details. He speaks of Drake's courtesy to him, and describes him as "a man about 35 years of age, low of stature, with a fair beard, and is one of the greatest mariners that sails the seas, both as a navigator and as a commander. His vessel...is manned with a hundred men....He treats them with affection, and they treat him with respect....He is served on silver dishes with gold borders and gilded garlands, in which are his arms....He dines and sups to the music of viols." Drake spoke to de Zarate of Doughty's execution, "speaking much good about the dead man, but adding that he had not been able to act otherwise, because this was what the Queen's service demanded. He showed me the commissions that he had received from her and carried....I managed to ascertain whether the general was well liked, and all said that they adored him."

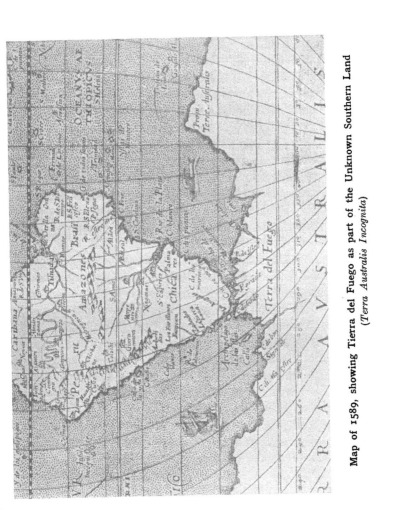

Map of 1589, showing Tierra del Fuego as part of the Unknown Southern Land
(*Terra Australis Incognita*)

the sole rights of sailing to the east of the Cape of Good Hope, or to the west through the Straits of Magellan, either to India or to any other country. One object of Le Maire and Schouten's expedition, which started from Holland in 1615, was to destroy this monopoly by discovering a new way to the Moluccas. In this they were successful, sailing into the Pacific through the strait (Le Maire Strait) between Staten Island and the mainland, and past Cape Horn, which they named after Hoorn, the town from which their ships came. When they reached Java, the President of the East India Company confiscated their vessel and cargo, refusing to believe that they had come by any other passage than the Straits of Magellan. Le Maire and Schouten were sent home in a ship of Speilbergen's fleet, but Le Maire died on the way. After two years of law-suits, Le Maire's father succeeded in proving his son's claim to the discovery of a new passage, and compelled the Dutch East India Company to return the ship and cargo, and to pay all costs and interest from the day of their seizure.

Another object of this expedition was the discovery of the supposed continent beyond Tierra del Fuego, in which some belief lingered, even after Drake's voyage. In this it was unsuccessful, and really disproved its existence. The discovery of the real great Unknown Southern Land—Australia—came later, though voyagers had already touched it.

NOTE. Pigafetta's account of Magellan's voyage is much abbreviated, by kind permission of the Hakluyt Society, from *The First Voyage Round the World by Magellan*, translated by Lord Stanley, 1874. Drake's and Cavendish's Voyages are taken from Hakluyt's *Principal Navigations, etc.*, and are practically complete. The passage from Le Maire and Schouten's voyage is from a translation by W. Phillip, published in 1619.

SOME IMPORTANT DATES IN THE HISTORY OF DISCOVERY

B.C.

327. Alexander the Great reaches India.

55. Julius Caesar visits Britain.

A.D.

861. The Vikings (under Naddod) discover Iceland.

877. Gunnbiorn discovers Greenland, which is colonised later by Eric the Red.

1000. Leif Ericson discovers Labrador (Helluland), Newfoundland (Markland) and Nova Scotia (Vinland). Colonies are founded, but afterwards abandoned.

1260–1271. Niccolo and Maffeo Polo (Marco Polo's father and uncle) go on a trading expedition through Asia to China.

1271–1295. Marco Polo goes with them on a second journey to the Court of Kublai Khan, and thence is sent as an envoy to Cochin China, India, etc.

1418–1460. Prince Henry of Portugal (Henry the Navigator) encourages discovery.

1420. Zarco discovers Madeira.

1455. Cadamosto reaches the Senegal and Cape Verde.

1484. Diego Cam discovers the Congo.

1486. Bartholomew Diaz rounds the Cape of Good Hope.

1492. Columbus discovers the West Indies.

1493. Columbus (2nd voyage) discovers Jamaica.

1497. Vasco da Gama reaches India by the Cape. On the way he sees Natal (Christmas Day), and Mozambique, and lands at Zanzibar.

1497. John Cabot re-discovers Newfoundland.

1498. Columbus (3rd voyage) discovers Trinidad and the Orinoco.

1499. Amerigo Vespucci discovers Venezuela (though great doubt is now cast on the accuracy of his statements).

1500. Pedro Cabral discovers Brazil.

1511. Serrano reaches the Moluccas (the Spice Islands).

1513. Balboa crosses the Isthmus of Panama, and sees the Pacific.

1789–93. Mackenzie discovers his river and British Columbia.
1792. Vancouver explores his island.
1796. Mungo Park reaches the Niger.
1797. Bass discovers his strait.
1799–1804. Humboldt explores South America.
1801–4. Flinders surveys the south coast of Australia.
1819–22. Franklin, Back and Richardson attempt the North-West Passage by land.
1819. Parry discovers Lancaster Sound.
1822. Denham and Clapperton discover Lake Tchad.
1828–31. Sturt traces the Darling and Murray Rivers.
1829–33. Ross attempts the North-West Passage, and discovers Boothia.
1840–42. Ross explores the Antarctic, and discovers Victoria Land, and the volcanoes Erebus and Terror (named after his ships).
1845–47. Franklin's last voyage.
1849–56. Livingstone explores the Zambesi, and discovers the Victoria Falls.
1850–54. M'Clure succeeds in the North-West Passage.
1858. Burton and Speke discover Lake Tanganyika, and Speke discovers Victoria Nyanza.
1858–62. Stuart crosses Australia from south to north.
1858–64. Livingstone explores Lake Nyasa.
1864. Baker discovers Albert Nyanza.
1873. Livingstone discovers Lake Moero.
1874–5. Cameron crosses equatorial Africa.
1876–7. Stanley explores the Congo River, and opens up Central Africa.
1878–79. Nordenskiöld succeeds in the North-East Passage.
1887–89. Stanley's expedition to rescue Emin Pasha. He discovers the Pigmies, and the Ruwenzori (the Mountains of the Moon).
1893–97. Nansen's voyage across the Arctic Ocean in the *Fram*. He reaches farthest north (86° 14′).
1909. Peary reaches the North Pole.
1911. Amundsen reaches the South Pole.
1912. Scott reaches the South Pole.

Ferdinand Magellan

FERDINAND MAGELLAN. THE FIRST VOYAGE ROUND THE WORLD (1519—1522)

By Antonio Pigafetta, patrician of Venice and Knight of Rhodes

Having heard that there was in the city of Seville, a small armada to the number of five ships, ready to perform this long voyage, that is to say, to find the islands of Maluco, from whence the spices come: of which armada the captain-general was Fernand de Magaglianes, a Portuguese gentleman, commander of *St James of the Sword*, who had performed several voyages in the ocean sea (in which he had behaved very honourably as a good man), I set out with many others in my favour from Barcelona, where at the time the Emperor was, and came by sea as far as Malaga, and thence I went away by land until I arrived at the said city of Seville. There I remained for the space of three months, waiting till the said armada was in order and readiness to perform its voyage. And because (very illustrious lord) that on the return from the said voyage, on going to Rome towards the holiness of our Holy Father, I found your lordship at Monterosa, where of your favour you gave me a good reception, and afterwards gave me to understand that you desired to have in writing the things which God of His grace had permitted me to see in my said voyage; therefore to satisfy and accede to your desire, I have reduced into this small book the principal things, in the best manner that I have been able.

Finally (very illustrious lord), after all provisions had been made, and the vessels were in order, the captain-general, a discreet and virtuous man, careful of his honour, would not commence his voyage without first making some good and wholesome ordinances, such as it is the good custom to make for those who go to sea. Nevertheless he did not entirely declare the voyage which he was going to make, so that his men should not from amazement and fear be unwilling to accompany him on so long a voyage, as he had undertaken in his intention. Considering the great and impetuous storms which are on the ocean sea, where I wished to go; and for another reason also, that is to say that the masters and captains of the other ships of his company did not love him: of this I do not know the reason, except by cause of his, the captain-general, being Portuguese, and they were Spaniards or Castilians, who for a long time have been in rivalry and ill will with one another. Notwithstanding this all were obedient to him. He made his ordinances such as those which follow, so that during the storms at sea, which often come on by night and day, his ships should not go away and separate from one another. These ordinances he published and made over in writing to each master of the ships, and commanded them to be observed and inviolably kept, unless there were great and legitimate excuses, and appearance of not having been able to do otherwise.

Firstly, the said captain-general willed that the vessel in which he himself was should go before the other vessels, and that the others should follow it; therefore he carried by night on the poop of his ship a torch or faggot of burning wood, which they called fanol, which burned all the night, so that his ships should not lose sight of him. Sometimes he set a lantern, sometimes a thick cord of reeds was lighted, which was called trenche. This is made of reeds well soaked in the water, and much beaten, then they are dried in the sun or in the smoke, and it is a thing very suitable for such a matter. When the captain had made one of his signals to his people, they answered in the same way. In that manner they knew whether the ships were following and keeping together or not. And when he wished to take a tack on account of the change of weather, or if the wind was contrary, or if he wished to make less way, he had two lights shown; and if he wished the others to lower their small sail, which was a part of the sail attached to the great sail, he showed three lights. Also by the three lights, notwithstanding that the wind was fair for going faster, he signalled that the studding sail should be lowered; so that the great sail might be quicker and more easily struck and furled when bad weather should suddenly set in, on account of some squall or otherwise. Likewise when the captain wished the other ships to lower the sail he had four lights shown, which shortly after he had put out and then showed a single one, which was a signal that he wished to stop there and turn, so that the other ships might do as he did. Withal, when he discovered any land, or shoal, that is to say, a rock at sea, he made several lights be shown or had a bombard fired off. If he wished to make sail, he signalled to the other ships with four lights, so that they should do as he did, and follow him. He always carried this said lantern suspended to the poop of his vessel. Also when he wished the studding sail to be replaced with the great sail, he showed three lights. And to know whether all the ships followed him and were coming together, he showed one light only besides the fanol, and then each of the ships showed another light, which was an answering signal.

Besides the above-mentioned ordinances for carrying on seamanship as is fitting, and to avoid the dangers which may come upon those who do not keep watch, the said captain, who was expert in the things required for navigation, ordered that three watches should be kept at night. The first was at the beginning of the night, the second at midnight, and the third towards break of day, which is commonly called *La diane*, otherwise the star of the break of day. Every night these watches were changed; that is to say, he who had kept the first watch, on the following day kept the second, and he who had kept the second kept the third; and so on they changed continually every night. The said captain commanded that his regulations both for the signals and the watches should be well observed, so that their voyage should be made with greater security. The crews of this fleet were divided into three companies; the first belonged to the captain, the second to the pilot or *nochier*, and the third to the master. These regulations having been made, the captain-general deliberated on sailing, as follows.

Monday, the day of St Laurence, the 10th of

August, in the year 1519, the fleet, provided with what was necessary for it, and carrying crews of different nations, to the number of two hundred and thirty-seven men in all the five ships, was ready to set sail from the mole of Seville.

Tuesday, the 20th September of the said year, we set sail from St Lucar, and on the twenty-sixth of the said month we arrived at an island of great Canaria, named Teneriphe, which is in twenty-eight degrees latitude; there we remained three days and a half to take in provisions and other things which were wanted. After that we set sail thence and came to a port named Monterose, where we sojourned two days to supply ourselves with pitch, which is a thing necessary for ships. It is to be known that among the other isles which are at the said great Canaria, there is one, where not a drop of water is to be found proceeding from a fountain or a river, only once a day at the hour of midday, there descends a cloud from the sky which envelops a large tree which is in this island, and it falls upon the leaves of the tree, and a great abundance of water distils from these leaves, so that at the foot of the tree there is so large a quantity of water that it seems as if there was an ever-running fountain. The men who inhabit this place are satisfied with this water; also the animals, both domestic and wild, drink of it.

Monday, the third of October of the said year, at the hour of midnight, we set sail, making the course auster, which the levantine mariners call Siroc, entering into the ocean sea. We passed the Cape Verd and the neighbouring islands in fourteen-and-a-half degrees, and we navigated for several days by the coast of Guinea or Ethiopia; where there is a mountain called Sierra Leona, which is in eight degrees latitude according to the art and science of cosmography and astrology. Sometimes we had the wind contrary and at other times sufficiently good, and rains without wind. In this manner we navigated with rain for the space of sixty days until the equinoctial line, which was a thing very strange and unaccustomed to be seen, according to the saying of some old men and those who had navigated here several times. Nevertheless, before reaching this equinoctial line we had in fourteen degrees a variety of weather and bad winds, as much on account of squalls as for the head winds and currents which came in such a manner that we could no longer advance. In order that our ships might not perish nor broach to (as it often happens when the squalls come together), we struck our sails, and in that manner we went about the sea hither and thither until the fair weather came. During the calm there came large fishes near the ships which they called *Tiburoni* (sharks), which have teeth of a terrible kind, and eat people when they find them in the sea either alive or dead. These fishes are caught with a device which the mariners call hamc, which is a hook of iron. Of these, some were caught by our men. However, they are worth nothing to eat when they are large; and even the small ones are worth but little. During these storms the body of St Anselm appeared to us several times; amongst others, one night that it was very dark on account of the bad weather, the said saint appeared in the form of a fire lighted at the summit of the mainmast, and remained there near two hours and a half, which comforted us greatly, for we were in tears, only expecting the hour of perishing; and when that holy light was going away from us it gave out so great a brilliancy in the eyes of each, that we were near a quarter-of-an-hour like people blinded, and calling out for mercy. For without any doubt nobody hoped to escape from that storm. It is to be noted that all and as many times as that light which represents the said St Anselm shows itself and descends upon a vessel which is in a storm at sea, that vessel never is lost. Immediately that this light had departed the sea grew calmer, and then we saw divers sorts of birds.

After that we had passed the equinoctial line, towards the south, we crossed as far as a country named Verzin, which is in twenty-four degrees and a half of the antarctic sky. This country is from the cape St Augustine, which is in eight degrees in the antarctic sky. At this place we had refreshments of victuals, like fowls and meat of calves, also a variety of fruits, called battate, pigne (pine-apples), sweet, of singular goodness, and many other things, which I have omitted mentioning, not to be too long. The people of the said place gave, in order to have a knife, or a hook for catching fish, five or six fowls, and for a comb they gave two geese, and for a small mirror, or a pair of scissors, they gave so much fish that ten men could have eaten of it. And for a bell (or hawk's-bell) they gave a full basket of the fruit named battate; this has the taste of a chestnut, and is of the length of a shuttle. For a king of cards, of that kind which they used to play with in Italy, they gave me five fowls, and thought they had cheated me. We entered into this port the day of Saint Lucy [13th December], before Christmas.

The said country of Verzin is very abundant in all good things, and is larger than France, Spain, and Italy together. It is one of the countries which the King of Portugal has conquered [acquired]. Its inhabitants are not Christians, and adore nothing, but live according to the usage of nature, rather bestially than otherwise. Some of these people live a hundred, or a hundred and twenty, or a hundred and forty years, and more; they go naked, both men and women. Their dwellings are houses that are rather long, and which they call "boy"; they sleep upon cotton nets, which they call, in their language, "amache." These nets are fastened to large timbers from one end of their house to the other. They make the fire to warm themselves right under their bed. It is to be known that in each of these houses, which they call "boy," there dwells a family of a hundred persons, who make a great noise. In this place they have boats, which are made of a tree, all in one piece, which they call "canoo." These are not made with iron instruments, for they have not got any, but with stones, like pebbles, and with these they plane and dig out these boats. Into these thirty or forty men enter, and their oars are made like iron shovels: and those who row these oars are black people, quite naked and shaven, and look like enemies of hell. The men and women of this said place are well made in their bodies. They eat the flesh of their enemies, not as good meat, but because they have adopted this custom.

I omit relating many other strange things, not to be too prolix; however, I will not forget to say that mass was said twice on shore, where there were many people of the said country, who remained on their knees, and their hands joined in great reverence, during the mass, so that it was a pleasure and a subject of compassion to see them. In a short time they built a house for us, as they imagined that we should remain a long time with them, and, at our departure thence, they gave us a large quantity of verzin. It is a colour which proceeds from the trees which are in this country, and they are in such quantity that the country is called from it Verzin.

We remained thirteen days in this country of Verzin, and, departing from it and following our course, we went as far as thirty-four degrees and a third towards the antarctic pole; there we found, near a river, men whom they call "cannibals," who eat human flesh, and one of these men, great as a giant, came to the captain's ship to ascertain and ask if the others might come. This man had a voice like a bull, and whilst this man was at the ship his companions carried off all their goods which they had to a castle further off, from fear of us. Seeing that, we landed a hundred men from the ships, and went after them to try and catch some others; however they gained in running away. This kind of people did more with one step than we could do at a bound. In this same river there were seven little islands, and in the largest of them precious stones are found. This place was formerly called the Cape of St Mary, and it was thought there that from thence there was a passage to the Sea of Sur; that is to say, the South Sea. And it is not found that any ship has ever discovered anything more, having passed beyond the said cape. And now it is no longer a cape, but it is a river which has a mouth seventeen leagues in width, by which it enters into the sea. In past time, in this river, these great men named

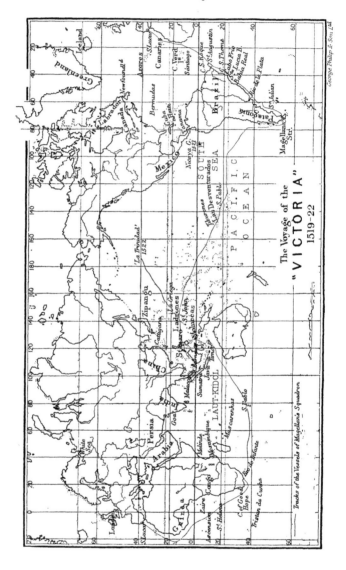

The Voyage of the "VICTORIA" 1519-22

Canibali ate a Spanish captain, named John de Solis, and sixty men who had gone to discover land, as we were doing, and trusted too much to them.

Afterwards following the same course towards the Antarctic pole, going along the land, we found two islands full of geese and goslings, and sea wolves, of which geese the large number could not be reckoned; for we loaded all the five ships with them in an hour. These geese are black, and have their feathers all over the body of the same size and shape, and they do not fly, and live upon fish; and they were so fat that they did not pluck them, but skinned them. They have beaks like that of a crow. The sea wolves of these two islands are of many colours, and of the size and thickness of a calf, and have a head like that of a calf, and the ears small and round. They have large teeth, and have no legs, but feet joining close on to the body, which resemble a human hand; they have small nails to their feet, and skin between the fingers like geese. If these animals could run they would be very bad and cruel, but they do not stir from the water, and swim and live upon fish. In this place we endured a great storm, and thought we should have been lost, but the three holy bodies, that is to say, St Anselm, St Nicolas, and St Clara, appeared to us, and immediately the storm ceased.

Departing thence as far as forty nine degrees and a half in the Antarctic heavens (as we were in the winter), we entered into a port to pass the winter, and remained there two whole months without ever seeing anybody. However, one day, without anyone expecting it, we saw a giant, who was on the shore of the sea, quite naked, and was dancing and leaping, and singing, and whilst singing he put the sand and dust on his head..

Our captain sent one of his men towards him, whom he charged to sing and leap like the other to reassure him, and show him friendship. This he did, and immediately the sailor led this giant to a little island where the captain was waiting for him; and when he was before us he began to be astonished, and to be afraid, and he raised one finger on high, thinking that we came from heaven. He was so tall that the tallest of us only came up to his waist; however he was well built. He had a large face, painted red all round, and his eyes also were painted yellow around them, and he had two hearts painted on his cheeks; he had but little hair on his head, and it was painted white. When he was brought before the captain he was clothed with the skin of a certain beast, which skin was very skilfully sewed. This beast has its head and ears of the size of a mule, and the neck and body of the fashion of a camel, the legs of a deer, and the tail like that of a horse, and it neighs like a horse. There is a great quantity of these animals in this same place. This giant had his feet covered with the skin of this animal in the form of shoes, and he carried in his hand a short and thick bow, with a thick cord made of the gut of the said beast, with a bundle of cane arrows, which were not very long, and were feathered like ours, but they had no iron at the end, though they had at the end some small white and black cut stones, and these arrows were like those which the Turks use. The captain caused food and drink to be given to this giant, then they showed him some things, amongst others, a steel mirror. When the giant saw his likeness in it, he was greatly terrified, leaping backwards, and made three or four of our men fall down.

After that the captain gave him two bells, a mirror, a comb, and a chaplet of beads, and sent him back on shore, having him accompanied by four armed men. One of the companions of this giant, who would never come to the ship, on seeing the other coming back with our people, came forward and ran to where the other giants dwelled. These came one after the other all naked, and began to leap and sing, raising one finger to heaven, and showing to our people a certain white powder made of the roots of herbs, which they kept in earthen pots, and they made signs that they lived on that, and that they had nothing else to eat than this powder.

Six days after, our people on going to cut wood, saw another giant, with his face painted and clothed like the above-mentioned. He had in his hand a bow and arrows, and approaching our people he made some touches on his head and then on his body, and afterwards did the same to our people. And this being done he raised both his hands to heaven. When the captain-general knew all this, he sent to fetch him with his ship's boat, and brought him to one of the little islands which are in the port, where the ships were. In this island the captain had caused a house to be made for putting some of the ships' things in whilst he remained there. This giant was of a still better disposition than the others, and was a gracious and amiable person, who liked to dance and leap. When he leapt he caused the earth to sink in a palm depth at the place where his feet touched. He was a long time with us, and at the end we baptised him, and gave him the name of John. This giant pronounced the name of Jesus, the Pater noster, Ave Maria, and his name as clearly as we did: but he had a terribly strong and loud voice. The captain gave him a shirt and a tunic of cloth, and seaman's breeches, a cap, a comb, some bells, and other things, and sent him back to where he had come from. He went away very joyous and satisfied.

Fifteen days later we saw four other giants, who carried no arrows, for they had hid them in the bushes, as two of them showed us, for we took them all four, and each of them was painted in a different way. The captain retained the two younger ones to take them to Spain on his return; but it was done by gentle and cunning means, for otherwise they would have done a hurt to some of our men. The manner in which he retained them was that he gave them many knives, forks, mirrors, bells, and glass, and they held all these things in their hands. Then the captain had some irons brought, such as are put on the feet of malefactors: these giants took pleasure in seeing the irons, but they did not know where to put them, and it grieved them that they could not take them with their hands, because they were hindered by the other things which they held in them. The other two giants were there, and were desirous of helping the other two, but the captain would not let them, and made a sign to the two whom he wished to detain that they would put those irons on their feet, and then they would go away: at this they made a sign with their heads that they were content. Immediately the captain had the irons put on the feet of both of them, and when they saw that they were striking with a hammer on the bolt which crosses the said irons to rivet them, and prevent them from being opened, these giants were afraid, but the captain made them a sign not to doubt of anything. Nevertheless when they saw the trick which had been played them, they began to be enraged, and to foam like bulls, crying out very loud Setebos, that is to say, the great devil, that he should help them. The hands of the other two giants were bound, but it was with great difficulty; then the captain sent them back on shore, with nine of his men to conduct them, and to bring the wife of one of those who had remained in irons, because he regretted her greatly, as we saw by signs. But in going away one of those two who were sent away, untied his hands and escaped, running with such lightness that our men lost sight of him, and he went away where his companions were staying; but he found nobody of those that he had left with the women because they had gone to hunt. However he went to look for them, and found them, and related to them all that had been done to them. The other giant whose hands were tied struggled as much as he could to unfasten himself, and to prevent his doing so, one of our men struck him, and hurt him on the head, at which he got very angry; however he led our people there where their wives were. Then John Cavagio, the pilot who was the chief conductor of these two giants, would not bring away the wife of one of the giants who had remained in irons on that evening, but was of opinion that they should sleep there, because it was almost night. During this time the one of the giants who had untied his hands came back from where he had been, with another giant, and they seeing their companion wounded on the head, said nothing at that moment, but next morning they spoke in their language to the women, and immediately all ran away together, and the smallest ran faster than the biggest, and they left all their chattels. Two of these giants being rather a long way off shot arrows at our men, and fighting thus, one of the giants pierced with an arrow the thigh of one of our men, of which he died immediately. Then seeing that he was dead, all ran away. Our men had cross-bows and guns, but they never could hit one of these giants, because they did not stand still in one place, but leaped hither and thither. After that, our men buried the man who had been killed, and set fire to the place where those giants had left their chattels. Certainly these giants run faster than a horse, and they are very jealous of their wives.

The captain named this kind of people Patagoni, who have no houses, but have huts made of the skins of the animals with which they clothe themselves, and go hither and thither with these huts of theirs, as the gypsies do; they live on raw meat, and eat a certain sweet root, which they call Capac. These two giants that we had in the ship ate a large basketful of biscuit, and rats without skinning them, and they drank half a bucket of water at each time.

We remained in this port, which was called the port of St Julian, about five months, during which there happened to us many strange things, of which I will tell a part. One was, that immediately that we entered into this port, the masters of the four other ships plotted treason against the captain-general, in order to put him to death. These were thus named: John of Carthagine, conductor of the fleet; the treasurer, Loys de Mendoza; the conductor, Anthony Cocha; and Gaspar de Quesada. However, the treason was discovered, for which the treasurer was killed with stabs of a dagger, and then quartered. This Gaspar de Quesada had his head cut off, and afterwards was cut into quarters; and the conductor having a few days later attempted another treason, was banished with a priest, and was put in that country called Patagonia. The captain-general would not put this conductor to death, because the Emperor Charles had made him captain of one of the ships. One of our ships, named *St James*, was lost in going to discover the coast; all the men, however, were saved by a miracle, for they were hardly wet at all.

We set up at the top of the highest mountain which was there a very large cross, as a sign that this country belonged to the King of Spain; and we gave to this mountain the name of Mount of Christ.

Departing thence, we found in fifty-one degrees less one-third (50° 40′ S.), in the Antarctic, a river of fresh water, which was near causing us to be lost, from the great winds which it sent out; but God, of his favour, aided us. We were about two months in this river, as it supplied fresh water and a kind of fish an ell long, and very scaly, which is good to eat. Before going away, the captain chose that all should confess and receive the body of our Lord like good Christians.

After going and taking the course to the fifty-second degree of the said Antarctic sky, on the day of the Eleven Thousand Virgins [October 21], we found, by a miracle, a strait which we called the Cape of the Eleven Thousand Virgins. This strait is a hundred and ten leagues long, which are four hundred and forty miles, and almost as wide as less than half a league, and it issues in another sea, which is called the peaceful sea; it is surrounded by very great and high mountains covered with snow. In this place it was not possible

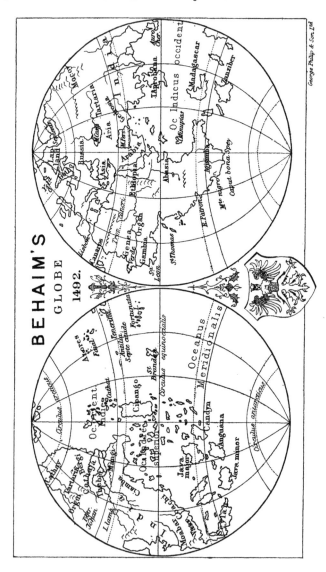

BEHAIM'S
GLOBE
1492.

to anchor with the anchors, because no bottom was found, on which account they were forced to put the moorings of twenty-five or thirty fathoms length on shore. This strait was a round place surrounded by mountains, as I have said, and the greater number of the sailors thought that there was no place by which to go out thence to enter into the peaceful sea. But the captain-general said that there was another strait for going out, and said that he knew it well, because he had seen it by a marine chart of the King of Portugal, which map had been made by a great pilot and mariner named Martin of Bohemia. The captain sent on before two of his ships, one named *St Anthony* and the other the *Conception*, to seek for and discover the outlet of this strait, which was called the Cape de la Baya. And we, with the other two ships, that is to say, the flagship named *Trinidad*, and the other the *Victory*, remained waiting for them within the Bay, where in the night we had a great storm, which lasted till the next day at midday, and during which we were forced to weigh the anchors and let the ships go hither and thither about the bay. The other two ships met with such a head wind that they could not weather a cape which the bay made almost at its extremity; wishing to come to us, they were near being driven to beach the ships. But, on approaching the extremity of the bay, and whilst expecting to be lost, they saw a small mouth, which did not resemble a mouth but a corner, and (like people giving up hope) they threw themselves into it, so that by force they discovered the strait. Seeing that it was not a corner, but a strait of land, they went further on and found a bay, then going still further they found another strait and another bay

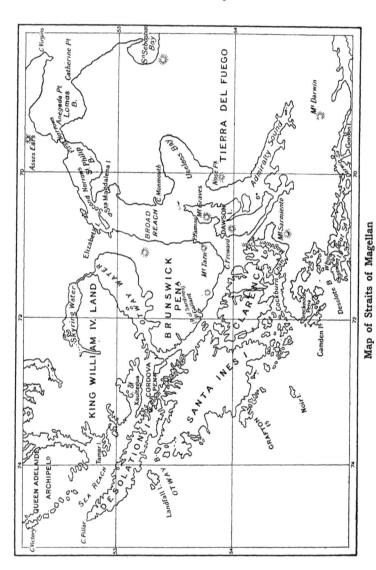

Map of Straits of Magellan

larger than the first two, at which, being very joyous, they suddenly returned backwards to tell it to the captain-general. Amongst us we thought that they had perished: first, because of the great storm; next, because two days had passed that we had not seen them. And being thus in doubt we saw the two ships under all sail, with ensigns spread, come towards us: these, when near us, suddenly discharged much artillery, at which we, very joyous, saluted them with artillery and shouts. Afterwards, all together, thanking God and the Virgin Mary, we went to seek further on.

After having entered inside this strait we found that there were two mouths, of which one trended to the Sirocco (S.E.), and the other to the Garbin (S.W.). On that account the captain again sent the two ships, *St Anthony* and *Conception*, to see if the mouth which was towards Sirocco had an outlet beyond into the said peaceful sea. One of these two ships, named *St Anthony*, would not wait for the other ship, because those who were inside wished to return to Spain: this they did, and the principal reason was on account of the pilot of the said ship being previously discontented with the said captain-general, because that before this armament was made, this pilot had gone to the Emperor to talk about having some ships to discover countries. But, on account of the arrival of the captain-general, the Emperor did not give them to this pilot, on account of which he agreed with some Spaniards, and the following night they took prisoner the captain of their ship, who was a cousin of the captain-general, and who was named Alvar de Meschite; they wounded him, and put him in irons. So they carried him off to Spain. And in this ship, which went away and returned, was

one of the two above-mentioned giants whom we had
taken, and when he felt the heat he died. The other
ship, named the *Conception*, not being able to follow
that one, was always waiting for it, and fluttered hither
and thither. But it lost its time, for the other took
the road by night for returning. When this happened,
at night the ship of the captain and the other ship went
together to discover the other mouth to Garbin (S.W.),
where, on always holding on our course, we found the
same strait. But at the end we arrived at a river
which we named the River of Sardines, because we
found a great quantity of them. So we remained
there four days to wait for the other two ships. A
short time after we sent a boat well supplied with men
and provisions to discover the cape of the other sea:
these remained three days in going and coming. They
told us that they had found the cape, and the sea great
and wide. At the joy which the captain-general had
at this he began to cry, and he gave the name of Cape
of Desire to this cape, as a thing which had been much
desired for a long time. Having done that we turned
back to find the two ships which were at the other
side, but we only found the *Conception*, of which ship
we asked what had become of her companion. To
this the captain of the said ship, named John Serrano
(who was pilot of the first ship which was lost, as has
been related), replied that he knew nothing of her, and
that he had never seen her since she entered the mouth.
However, we sought for her through all the strait, as
far as the said mouth, by which she had taken her
course to return. Besides that, the captain-general
sent back the ship named the *Victory* as far as the
entrance of the strait to see if the ship was there, and

he told the people of this ship that if they did not find the ship they were looking for, they were to place an ensign on the summit of a small hill, with a letter inside a pot placed in the ground near the ensign, so that if the ship should by chance return, it might see that ensign, and also find the letter which would give information of the course which the captain was holding. This manner of acting had been ordained by the captain from the commencement, in order to effect the junction of any ship which might be separated from the others. So the people of the said ship did what the captain had commanded them, and more, for they set two ensigns with letters; one of the ensigns was placed on a small hill at the first bay, the other on an islet in the third bay, where there were many sea wolves and large birds. The captain-general waited for them with the other ship near the river named Isles: and he caused a cross to be set upon a small island in front of that river, which was between high mountains covered with snow. This river comes and falls into the sea near the other river of the Sardines.

If we had not found this strait the captain-general had made up his mind to go as far as seventy-five degrees towards the antarctic pole; where at that height in the summer time there is no night, or very little: in a similar manner in the winter there is no day-light, or very little, and so that every one may believe this, when we were in this strait the night lasted only three hours, and this was in the month of October.

The land of this strait on the left hand side looked towards the Sirocco wind, which is the wind collateral to the Levant and South; we called this strait Pathagonico. In it we found at every half league a good port and place for anchoring, good waters, wood all of cedar, and fish like sardines, missiglioni, and a very sweet herb named appio (celery). There is also some of the same kind which is bitter. This herb grows near the springs, and from not finding anything else we ate of it for several days. I think that there is not in the world a more beautiful country, or better strait than this one. In this ocean sea one sees a very amusing chase of fish, which are of three sorts, of an ell or more in length, and they call these fish Dorades, Albacores, and Bonitos; these follow and pursue another sort of fish which flies, which they call Colondriny, which are a foot long or more, and are very good to eat. When these three sorts of fish find in the water any of these flying fish, immediately they make them comè out of the water, and they fly more than a crossbow-shot, as long as their wings are wet; and whilst these fishes fly the other three run after them under the water, seeing the shadow of those that fly: and the moment they fall into the water they are seized upon and eaten by the others which pursue them, which is a thing marvellous and agreeable to see.

Wednesday, the twenty-eighth of November, 1520, we came forth out of the said strait, and entered into the Pacific sea, where we remained three months and twenty days without taking in provisions or other refreshments, and we only ate old biscuit reduced to powder, and full of grubs, and stinking from the dirt which the rats had made on it when eating the good biscuit, and we drank water that was yellow and stinking. We also ate the ox hides which were under the main-yard, so that the yard should not break the

Magellan passing his Strait

rigging: they were very hard on account of the sun, rain, and wind, and we left them for four or five days in the sea, and then we put them a little on the embers, and so ate them; also the sawdust of wood, and rats which cost half-a-crown each, moreover enough of them were not to be got. Besides the above-named evils, this misfortune which I will mention was the worst, it was that the upper and lower gums of most of our men grew so much that they could not eat, and in this way so many suffered, that nineteen died, and the other giant, and an Indian from the country of Verzin. Besides those who died, twenty-five or thirty fell ill of divers sicknesses, both in the arms and legs, and other places, in such manner that very few remained healthy. However, thanks be to the Lord, I had no sickness. During those three months and twenty days we went in an open sea, while we ran fully four thousand leagues in the Pacific sea. This was well named Pacific, for during this same time we met with no storm, and saw no land except two small uninhabited islands, in which we found only birds and trees. We named them the Unfortunate Islands; they are two hundred leagues apart from one another, and there is no place to anchor, as there is no bottom. There we saw many sharks, which are a kind of large fish which they call Tiburoni. The first isle is in fifteen degrees of austral latitude, and the other island is in nine degrees. With the said wind we ran each day fifty or sixty leagues, or more; now with the wind astern, sometimes on a wind or otherwise. And if our Lord and his Mother had not aided us in giving us good weather to refresh ourselves with provisions and other things, we should all have died of hunger in this very vast sea, and I think that never man will undertake to perform such a voyage.

On Wednesday, the 6th of March, we discovered a small island in the north-west direction, and two others lying to the south-west. One of these islands was larger and higher than the other two. The captain-general wished to touch at the largest of these three islands to get refreshments of provisions; but it was not possible because the people of these islands entered into the ships and robbed us, in such a way that it was impossible to preserve oneself from them. Whilst we were striking and lowering the sails to go ashore, they stole away with much address and diligence the small boat called the skiff, which was made fast to the poop of the captain's ship, at which he was much irritated, and went on shore with forty armed men, burned forty or fifty houses, with several small boats, and killed seven men of the island; they recovered their skiff.

Immediately after we sailed from that island, following our course, and those people seeing that we were going away followed us for a league, with a hundred small boats, or more, and they approached our ships, showing to us fish, and feigning to give it to us. But they threw stones at us, and then ran away, and in their flight they passed with their little boats between the boat which is towed at the poop and the ship going under full sail; but they did this so quickly, and with such skill that it was a wonder.

These people have no arms, but use sticks, which have a fish bone at the end. They are poor, but ingenious, and great thieves, and for the sake of that we called these three islands the Ladrone Islands.

Saturday, the 16th of March, 1521, we arrived at daybreak in sight of a high island, three hundred leagues distant from the before-mentioned Thieves' island. This isle is named Zamal. The next day the captain-general wished to land at another uninhabited island near the first, to be in greater security and to take water, also to repose there a few days. He set up there two tents on shore for the sick, and had a sow killed for them.

Monday, the 18th of March, after dinner, we saw a boat come towards us with nine men in it: upon which the captain-general ordered that no one should move or speak without his permission. When these people had come into this island towards us, immediately the principal one amongst them went towards the captain-general with demonstrations of being very joyous at our arrival. Five of the most showy of them remained with us, the others who remained with the boat went to call some men who were fishing, and afterwards all of them came together. The captain seeing that these people were reasonable, ordered food and drink to be given them, and he gave them some red caps, looking-glasses, combs, bells, ivory, and other things. When these people saw the politeness of the captain, they presented some fish, and a vessel of palm wine, which they call in their language Uraca; figs more than a foot long, and others smaller and of a better savour, and two cocos. At that time they had nothing to give him, and they made signs to us with their hands that in four days they would bring us Umai, which is rice, cocos, and many other victuals.

To explain the kind of fruits above-named it must be known that the one which they call coco, is the

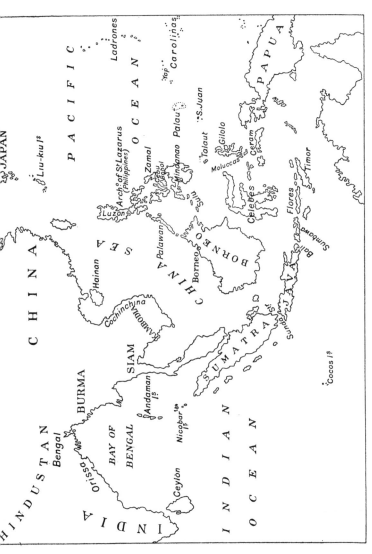

Map of the East Indies

fruit which the palm trees bear. And as we have
bread, wine, oil, and vinegar, proceeding from different
kinds, so these people have those things proceeding
from these palm trees only. It must be said that wine
proceeds from the said palm trees in the following
manner. They make a hole at the summit of the tree
as far as its heart, which is named palmito, from which
a liquor comes out in drops down the tree, like white
must, which is sweet, but with somewhat of bitter.
They have canes as thick as the leg, in which they
draw off this liquor, and they fasten them to the tree
from the evening till next morning, and from the
morning to the evening, because this liquor comes
little by little. This palm produces a fruit named
coco, which is as large as the head, or thereabouts:
its first husk is green, and two fingers in thickness: in
it they find certain threads, with which they make the
cords for fastening their boats. Under this husk there
is another very hard, and thicker than that of a walnut.
They burn this second rind, and make with it a powder
which is useful to them. Under this rind there is a
white marrow of a finger's thickness, which they eat
fresh with meat and fish, as we do bread, and it has
the taste of an almond, and if anyone dried it he might
make bread of it. From the middle of this marrow
there comes out a clear sweet water, and very cordial,
which, when it has rested a little, and settled, congeals
and becomes like an apple. When they wish to make
oil they take this fruit, the coco, and let it get rotten,
and they corrupt this marrow in the water, then they
boil it, and it becomes oil in the manner of butter.
When they want to make vinegar, they let the water
in the coco-nut get bad, and they put it in the sun,

when it turns to vinegar like white wine. From this fruit milk also can be made, as we experienced, for we scraped this marrow and then put it with its water, and passed it through a cloth, and thus it was milk like that of goats. This kind of palm tree is like the date-palm, but not so rugged. Two of these trees can maintain a family of ten persons: but they do not draw wine as above-mentioned always from one tree, but draw from one for eight days, and from the other as long. For if they did not, otherwise the trees would dry up.

We remained at this place eight days: the captain went there every day to see his sick men, whom he had placed on this island to refresh them: and he gave them himself every day the water of this said fruit the coco, which comforted them much.

The Monday of Passion week, the 25th of March, and feast of our Lady, in the afternoon, and being ready to depart from this place, I went to the side of our ship to fish, and putting my feet on a spar to go down to the store room, my feet slipped, because it had rained, and I fell into the sea without any one seeing me, and being near drowning by luck I found at my left hand the sheet of the large sail which was in the sea, I caught hold of it and began to cry out till they came to help and pick me up with the boat. I was assisted not by my merits, but by the mercy and ‧grace of the fountain of pity. That same day we took the course between west and south-west, and passed amidst four small islands, that is to say, Cenalo, Huinanghar, Ibusson, and Abarien.

Thursday, the 28th of March, having seen the night before fire upon an island, at the morning we came to

anchor at this island; where we saw a small boat
which they call boloto, with eight men inside, which
approached the ship of the captain-general. Then a
slave of the captain's, who was from Sumatra, otherwise named Taprobana, spoke from afar to these
people, who understood his talk, and came near to
the side of the ship, but they withdrew immediately,
and would not enter the ship from fear of us. So the
captain seeing that they would not trust to us showed
them a red cap, and other things, which he had tied
and placed on a little plank, and the people in the boat
took them immediately and joyously, and then returned
to advise their king. Two hours afterwards, or thereabouts, we saw come two long boats, which they call
balangai, full of men. In the largest of them was
their king sitting under an awning of mats; when they
were near the ship of the captain-general, the said slave
spoke to the king, who understood him well, because in
these countries the kings know more languages than
the common people. Then the king ordered some of
his people to go to the captain's ship, whilst he would
not move from his boat, which was near enough to us.
This was done, and when his people returned to the
boat, he went away at once. The captain gave good
entertainment to the men who came to his ship, and
gave them all sorts of things, on which account the
king wished to give the captain a rather large bar of
solid gold, and a chest full of ginger. However, the
captain thanked him very much but would not accept
the present. After that, when it was late, we went
with the ships near to the houses and abode of the king.

The next day which was Good Friday, the captain
sent on shore the before-mentioned slave, who was our

interpreter, to the king to beg him to give him for money some provisions for his ships, sending him word that he had not come to his country as an enemy, but as a friend. The king on hearing this came with seven or eight men in a boat, and entered the ship, and embraced the captain, and gave him three china dishes covered with leaves full of rice, and two *dorades*, which are rather large fish, and of the sort above-mentioned, and he gave him several other things. The captain gave this king a robe of red and yellow cloth, made in the Turkish fashion, and a very fine red cap, and to his people he gave to some of them knives, and to others mirrors. After that refreshments were served up to them. The captain told the king, through the said interpreter, that he wished to be with him, *cassi cassi*, that is to say, brothers. To which the king answered that he desired to be the same towards him. After that the captain showed him cloths of different colours, linen, coral, and much other merchandise, and all the artillery, of which he had some pieces fired before him, at which the king was much astonished; after that the captain had one of his soldiers armed with white armour, and placed him in the midst of three comrades, who struck him with swords and daggers. The king thought this very strange, and the captain told him, through the interpreter, that a man thus in white armour was worth a hundred of his men; he answered that it was true; he was further informed that there were in each ship two hundred like that man. After that the captain showed him a great number of swords, cuirasses, and helmets, and made two of the men play with their swords before the king; he then showed him the sea chart and the ship compass, and

informed him how he had found the strait to come
there, and of the time which he had spent in coming;
also of the time he had been without seeing any land,
at which the king was astonished. At the end the
captain asked if he would be pleased that two of his
people should go with him to the places where they
lived, to see some of the things of his country. This
the king granted, and I went with another.

When I had landed, the king raised his hands to
the sky, and turned to us two, and we did the same
as he did; after that he took me by the hand, and
one of his principal people took my companion, and
led us under a place covered with canes, where there
was a balangai, that is to say, a boat, eighty feet
long or thereabouts, resembling a fusta. We sat with
the king upon its poop, always conversing with him by
signs, and his people stood up around us, with their
swords, spears, and bucklers. Then the king ordered
to be brought a dish of pig's flesh and wine. Their
fashion of drinking is in this wise—they first raise their
hands to heaven, then take the drinking vessel in their
right hand, and extend the left hand closed towards
the people. This the king did, and presented to me
his fist, so that I thought that he wanted to strike me;
I did the same thing towards him; so with this ceremony, and other signs of friendship, we banqueted,
and afterwards supped with him.

I ate flesh on Good Friday, not being able to do
otherwise, and before the hour of supper, I gave
several things to the king, which I had brought.
There I wrote down several things as they name them
in their language, and when the king and the others
saw me write, and I told them their manner of speech,

they were all astonished. When the hour for supper had come, they brought two large china dishes, of which one was full of rice, and the other of pig's flesh, with its broth and sauce. We supped with the same signs and ceremonies, and then went to the king's palace, which was made and built like a hay grange, covered with fig and palm leaves. It was built on great timbers high above the ground, and it was necessary to go up steps and ladders to it. Then the king made us sit on a cane mat, with our legs doubled as was the custom; after half an hour there was brought a dish of fish roast in pieces, and ginger fresh gathered that moment, and some wine. The eldest son of the king, who was the prince, came where we were, and the king told him to sit down near us, which he did; then two dishes were brought, one of fish, with its sauce, and the other of rice, and this was done for us to eat with the prince. My companion enjoyed the food and drink so much that he got drunk. They use for candles or torches the gum of a tree which is named Animé, wrapped up in leaves of palms or fig trees. The king made a sign that he wished to go to rest, and left with us the prince, with whom we slept on a cane mat, with some cushions and pillows of leaves. Next morning the king came and took me by the hand, and so we went to the place where we had supped, to breakfast, but the boat came to fetch us. The king, before we went away, was very gay, and kissed our hands, and we kissed his. There came with us a brother of his, the king of another island, accompanied by three men. The captain-general detained him to dine with us, and we gave him several things.

In the island belonging to the king who came to the ship there are mines of gold, which they find in pieces as big as a walnut or an egg, by seeking in the ground. All the vessels which he makes use of are made of it, and also some parts of his house, which was well fitted up according to the custom of the country, and he was the handsomest man that we saw among these nations. He had very black hair coming down to his shoulders, with a silk cloth on his head, and two large gold rings hanging from his ears, he had a cloth of cotton worked with silk, which covered him from the waist to the knees, at his side he wore a dagger, with a long handle which was all of gold, its sheath was of carved wood. Besides he carried upon him scents of storax and benzoin. He was tawny and painted all over. The island of this king is named Zuluan and Calagan, and when these two kings wish to visit one another they come to hunt in this island where we were. Of these kings the painted king is called Raja Calambu, and the other Raja Siani.

On Sunday, the last day of March, and feast of Easter, the captain sent the chaplain ashore early to say mass, and the interpreter went with him to tell the king that they were not coming on shore to dine with him, but only to hear the mass. The king hearing that sent two dead pigs. When it was time for saying mass the captain went ashore with fifty men, not with their arms, but only with their swords, and dressed as well as each one was able to dress, and before the boats reached the shore our ships fired six cannon shots as a sign of peace. At our landing the two kings were there, and received our captain in a friendly manner, and placed him between them, and

then we went to the place prepared for saying mass,
which was not far from the shore. Before the mass
began the captain threw a quantity of musk rose water
on those two kings, and when the offertory of the mass
came, the two kings went to kiss the cross like us, but
they offered nothing, and at the elevation of the body
of our Lord they were kneeling like us, and adored our
Lord with joined hands. The ships fired all their
artillery at the elevation of the body of our Lord.
After mass had been said each one did the duty of a
Christian, receiving our Lord. After that the captain
had some sword-play by his people, which gave great
pleasure to the kings. Then he had a cross brought,
with the nails and crown, to which the kings made
reverence, and the captain had them told that these
things which he showed them were the sign of the
emperor his lord and master, from whom he had
charge and commandment to place it in all places
where he might go or pass by. He told them that
he wished to place it in their country for their profit,
because if there came afterwards any ships from Spain
to those islands, on seeing this cross, they would know
that we had been there, and therefore they would not
cause them any displeasure to their persons nor their
goods; and if they took any of their people, on showing
them this sign, they would at once let them go.
Besides this, the captain told them that it was necessary
that this cross should be placed on the summit of the
highest mountain in their country, so that seeing it
every day they might adore it, and that if they did
thus, neither thunder, lightning, nor the tempest could
do them hurt. The kings thanked the captain, and
said they would do it willingly. Then he asked

whether they were Moors or Gentiles, and in what
they believed. They answered that they did not perform any other adoration, but only joined their hands,
looking up to heaven, and that they called their God,
Aba. Hearing this, the captain was very joyful: on
seeing that, the first king raised his hands to the sky
and said that he wished it were possible for him to be
able to show the affection which he felt towards him.
The interpreter asked him for what reason there was
so little to eat in that place, to which the king replied
that he did not reside in that place except when he
came to hunt and to see his brother, but that he lived
in another island where he had all his family. Then
the captain asked him if he had any enemies who
made war upon him, and that if he had any he would
go and defeat them with his men and ships, to put
them under his obedience. The king thanked him,
and answered that there were two islands the inhabitants of which were his enemies; however, that for
the present it was not the time to attack them. The
captain therefore said to him that if God permitted
him to return another time to this country, he would
bring so many men that he would put them by force
under his obedience. Then he bade the interpreter
tell them that he was going away to dine, and after
that he would return to place the cross on the summit
of the mountain. The two kings said they were content, and on that they embraced the captain, and he
separated from them.

After dinner we all returned in our dress coats, and
we went together with the two kings to the middle of
the highest mountain we could find, and there the
cross was planted. After that the two kings and the

captain rested themselves; and, while conversing, I asked where was the best port for obtaining victuals. They replied that there were three, that is to say, Ceylon, Zubu, and Calagan, but that Zubu was the largest and of the most traffic. Then the kings offered to give him pilots to go to those ports, for which he thanked them, and deliberated to go there, for his ill-fortune would have it so. After the cross had been planted on that mountain, each one said the Paternoster and Ave Maria, and adored it, and the kings did the like. Then we went down below to where their boats were. There the kings had brought some of the fruit called cocos and other things to make a collation and to refresh us. The captain, being desirous to depart the next day in the morning, asked the king for the pilots to conduct us to the above-mentioned ports, promising him to treat them like themselves, and that he would leave one of his own men as a hostage. The first king said that he would go himself and conduct him to this port, and be his pilot, but that he should wait two days, until he had had his rice gathered in and done other things which he had to do, begging him to lend him some of his men so as to get done sooner. This the captain agreed to.

This island is named Mazzava. We remained seven days in this place.

Sunday, the 7th of April, about midday, we entered the port of Zubu, having passed by many villages.

The king bade one of his principal men ask what we were seeking. The interpreter answered him that his master was captain of the greatest king in the world, and that he was going by the command of the said sovereign to discover the Molucca islands. However, on account of what he had heard where he had passed, and especially from the King of Mazzava, of his courtesy and good fame, he had wished to pass by his country to visit him, and also to obtain some refreshment of victuals for his merchandise.

Then the king answered that he would speak to his council, and give an answer the next day. Afterwards the king ordered a collation to be brought of several viands, all of meat, in porcelain dishes, with a great many vessels of wine. When the repast was over, our people returned, and related all to the captain; and the King of Mazzava, who was on board the captain's ship, and who was the first king after him of Zubu, and the lord of several isles, wished to go on shore to relate to the king the politeness and courtesy of our captain.

Monday morning our clerk went with the interpreter to the town of Zubu, and the king, accompanied by the principal men of his kingdom, came to the open space, where we made our people sit down near him, and he asked whether there was more than one captain in all those ships, and whether he wished that the king should pay tribute to the emperor, his master : to which our people answered, no, but that the captain only wished to trade with the things which he had brought with the people of his country, and not with others. Then the king said that he was content, and as a greater sign of affection he sent him a little of his blood from his right arm, and wished he should do the like. Our people answered that he would do it. Besides that, he said that all the captains who came to his country had been accustomed to make a present to him, and he to them, and therefore they should ask their captain if he would observe the custom. Our people answered that he would; but as the king wished to keep up the custom, let him begin and make a present, and then the captain would do his duty.

Tuesday morning following the King of Mazzava, with a Moor, came to the ship, and saluted the captain on behalf of the King of Zubu, and said that the king was preparing a quantity of provisions, as much as he could, to make a present of to him, and that after dinner he would send two of his nephews, with others of his principal people, to make peace with him. Then the captain had one of his men armed with his own armour, and told him that all of us would fight armed in that manner, at which the Moorish merchant was rather astonished; but the captain told him not to be afraid, and that our arms were soft to our friends and rough to our enemies; and that as a cloth wipes away the sweat from a man, so our arms destroy the enemies of our faith. The captain said this to the Moor, because he was more intelligent than the others, and for him to relate it all to the King of Zubu.

After dinner, the nephew of this king, who was a prince, with the King of Mazzava, the Moor, the governor, and the chief of police, and eight of the principal men, came to the ship to make peace with us. The captain-general was sitting in a chair of red velvet, and near him were the principal men of the ships sitting in leather chairs, and the others on the ground on mats. Then the captain bade the interpreter ask the above-mentioned persons if it was their custom to speak in secret or in public, and whether the prince who was come with them had power to conclude peace. They answered yes, that they would speak in public, and that they had the power to conclude peace. The captain spoke at length on the subject of peace, and prayed God to confirm it in heaven. These people replied that they had never heard such words as these which the captain had spoken to them, and they took great pleasure in hearing them. The captain, seeing then that those people listened willingly to what was said to them, and that they gave good answers, began to say a great many more good things to induce them to become Christians.

The people heard these things willingly, and besought the captain to leave them two men to teach and show them the Christian faith, and they would entertain them well with great honour. To this the captain answered that for the moment he could not leave them any of his people, but that if they wished to be Christians that his priest would baptise them, and that another time he would bring priests and preachers to teach them the faith. They then answered that they wished first to speak to their king, and then would become Christians. Each of us wept for the joy which we felt at the goodwill of these people, and the captain told them not to become Christians from fear of us, or to please us, but that if they wished to become Christian they must do it willingly, and for the love of God, for even though they should not become Christian, no displeasure would be done them, but those who became Christian would be more loved and better treated than the others. Then they all cried out with one voice, that they did not wish to become Christian from fear, nor from complaisance, but of their free will. The captain then said that if they became Christians he would leave them the arms which the Christians use, and that his king had commanded him so to do. At last they said they did not know what more to answer to so many good and beautiful words which he spoke to them, but that they placed themselves in his hands, and that he should do with them as with his own servants. Then the captain, with tears in his eyes, embraced them, and, taking the hand of the prince and that of the king, said to him that by the faith he had in God, and to his master the emperor, and by the habit of St James which he wore, he promised them to cause them to have perpetual peace with the King of Spain, at which the prince and the others promised him the same. After peace had been concluded, the captain had refreshments served to them. The prince and the King of Mazzava, who was with him, presented to the captain on behalf of his king large baskets full of rice, pigs, goats, and fowls, and desired the captain to be told he should pardon them that their present was not as fine as was fitting for him. The captain gave to the prince some very fine cloth and a red cap, and a quantity of glass and a cup of gilt glass. Glasses are much prized in this country. To the other people belonging to the Prince he gave various things. Then he sent by me and another person to the King of Zubu a robe of yellow and violet silk in the fashion of a Turkish jubbeh, a red cap, very fine, and certain pieces of glass, and had all of them put in a silver dish, and two gilt glasses.

When we came to the town we found the King of Zubu at his palace, sitting on the ground on a mat made of palm, with many people about him. He was quite naked, except that he had a cloth round his middle, and a loose wrapper round his head, worked with silk by the needle. He had a very heavy chain round his neck, and two gold rings hung in his ears with precious stones. He was a small and fat man, and his face was painted with fire in different ways. He was eating on the ground on another palm mat, and was then eating tortoise eggs in two china dishes, and he had four vessels full of palm wine, which he drank with a cane pipe. We made our obeisance, and presented to him what the captain had sent him, and told him through the interpreter that it was not as a return for his present which he had sent to the captain, but for the affection which he bore him. That done, his people told him all the good words and explanations of peace and religion which he had spoken to them. The king wished to detain us to supper, but we made our excuses and took leave of him. The prince, nephew of the king, conducted us to his house, and showed us four girls who played on four instruments, which were strange and very soft, and their manner of playing is rather musical. Afterwards he made us dance with them.

Saturday following a scaffolding was made in the open space, fitted with tapestry and palm branches, because the king had promised our captain to become Christian on Sunday. He told him not to be afraid when our artillery fired on that day, for it was the custom to load it on those feasts without firing stones or other balls.

Sunday morning, the fourteenth day of April, we went on shore, forty men, of whom two were armed, who marched before us, following the standard of our king emperor. When we landed the ships discharged all their artillery, and from fear of it the people ran away in all directions. The captain and the king embraced one another, and then joyously we went near the scaffolding, where the captain and the king sat on two chairs, one covered with red, the other with violet velvet. The principal men sat on cushions, and the others on mats, after the fashion of the country. Then the captain began to speak to the king through the interpreter to incite him to the faith of Jesus Christ, and told him that if he wished to be a good Christian, as he had said the day before, that he must burn all the idols of his country, and, instead of them, place a cross, and that everyone should worship it every day on their knees, and their hands joined to heaven : and he showed him how he ought every day to make the sign of the cross. To that the king and all his people answered that they would obey the commands of the captain and do all that he told them. The captain took the king by the hand, and they walked about on the scaffolding, and when he was baptised he said that he would name him Don Charles, as the emperor his sovereign was named ; and he named the prince Don Fernand, after the brother of the emperor, and the King of Mazzava Jehan : to the Moor he gave the name of Christopher, and to the others each a name of his fancy. Thus, before mass, there were fifty men baptised. After mass had been heard the captain invited the king and his other principal men to dine with him, but he would not. He accompanied the captain, however, to the beach, and on his arrival there the ships fired all their artillery. Then, embracing one another, they took leave.

After dinner our chaplain and some of us went on shore to baptise the queen. She came with forty ladies, and we conducted them on to the scaffolding; then made her sit down on a cushion, and her women around her, until the priest was ready. During that time they showed her an image of our Lady, of wood, holding her little child, which was very well made, and a cross. When she saw it, she had a greater desire to be a Christian, and, asking for baptism, she was baptised and named Jehanne, like the mother of the emperor. The wife of the prince, daughter of this queen, had the name of Catherine, the Queen of Mazzava Isabella, and the others each their name. That day we baptised eight hundred persons of men, women, and children. The Queen was young and handsome, covered with a black and white sheet; she had the mouth and nails very red, and wore on her head a large hat made of leaves of palm, with a crown over it made of the same leaves, like that of the Pope. After that she begged us to give her the little wooden boy to put in the place of the idols. This we did, and she went away. In the evening the king and queen, with several of their people, came to the sea beach, where the captain had some of the large artillery fired, in which they took great pleasure. The captain and the king called one another brother.

At last, in eight days, all the inhabitants of this island were baptised, and some belonging to the neighbouring islands. In one of these we burned a village because the inhabitants would not obey either the king or us. There we planted a cross because the people were Gentiles: if they had been Moors, we should have erected a column, as a sign of their hardness of heart, because the Moors are more difficult to convert than the Gentiles. The captain-general went ashore every day to hear mass, to which there came many of the new Christians, to whom he explained various points of our religion. One day the queen came with all her state. She was preceded by three damsels, who carried in their hands three of her hats: she was dressed in black and white, with a large silk veil with gold stripes, which covered her head and shoulders. Very many women followed her, with their heads covered with a small veil, and a hat above that: the rest of their bodies and feet were naked, except a small wrapper of palm cloth which covered their middles. Their hair fell flowing over their shoulders. The queen, after making a bow to the altar, sat upon a cushion of embroidered silk, and the captain sprinkled over her and over some of her ladies rose water and musk, a perfume which pleases the ladies of this country very much. The captain on that occasion approved of the gift which I had made to the queen of the image of the Infant Jesus, and recommended her to put it in the place of her idols, because it was a remembrancer of the Son of God. She promised to do all this, and to keep it with much care.

The captain-general, who had informed the king and all those who had been baptised of the obligation they were under of burning their idols, which they had promised to do, seeing that they retained them and made them offerings of meat, reproved them severely for it. They thought to excuse themselves sufficiently by saying that they did not do that now on their own account, but for a sick person, for the idols to restore him his health. This sick man was a brother of the prince, and was reputed to be the most valiant and wise man in the island, and his illness was so severe that for four days he had not spoken. Having heard this, the captain, seized with zeal for religion, said that if they had a true faith in Jesus Christ, they should burn all the idols, and the sick man should be baptised, and he would be immediately cured, of which he was so certain that he consented to lose his head if the miracle did not take place. The king promised that all this should be done, because he truly believed in Jesus Christ. Then we arranged, with all the pomp that was possible, a procession from the place to the house of the sick man. We went there, and indeed found him unable to speak or to move. We baptised him, with two of his wives and ten girls. The captain then asked him how he felt, and he at once spoke, and said that by the grace of Our Lord he was well enough. This great miracle was done under our eyes. The captain, on hearing him speak, gave great thanks to God. He gave him a refreshing drink to take, and afterwards sent to his house a mattress, two sheets, a covering of yellow wool, and a cushion, and he continued to send him, until he was quite well, refreshing drinks of almonds, rosewater, rosoglio, and some sweet preserves.

On the fifth day the convalescent rose from his bed, and as soon as he could walk, he had burned, in the presence of the king and of all the people, an idol which some old women had concealed in his house. He also caused to be destroyed several temples constructed on the sea shore, in which people were accustomed to eat the meat offered to the idols. The inhabitants applauded this, and, shouting "Castile, Castile," helped to throw them down, and declared that if God gave them life they would burn all the idols they could find, even if they were in the king's own house.

These idols are made of wood, they are concave or hollowed out behind, they have the arms and legs spread out, and the feet turned upwards; they have a large face, with four very large teeth like those of a wild boar, and they are all painted.

Friday, the 26th of April, Zula, who was one of the principal men or chiefs of the island of Matan, sent to the captain a son of his with two goats to make a present of them, and to say that if he did not do all that he had promised, the cause of that was another chief named Silapulapu, who would not in any way obey the King of Spain, and had prevented him from doing so: but that if the captain would send him the following night one boat full of men to give him assistance, he would fight and subdue his rival. On the receipt of this message, the captain decided to go himself with three boats. We entreated him much not to go to this enterprise in person, but he as a good shepherd would not abandon his flock.

We set out from Zubu at midnight, we were sixty men armed with corslets and helmets; there were with us the Christian king, the prince, and some of the chief men, and many others divided among twenty or thirty balangai. We arrived at Matan three hours before daylight. The captain before attacking wished to attempt gentle means, and sent on shore the Moorish merchant to tell those islanders who were of the party of Silapulapu, that if they would recognise the Christian king as their sovereign, and obey the King of Spain, and pay us the tribute which had been asked, the

captain would become their friend, otherwise we should
prove how our lances wounded. The islanders were
not terrified: they replied that if we had lances, so also
had they, although only of reeds, and wood hardened
with fire. They asked however that we should
not attack them by night, but wait for daylight,
because they were expecting reinforcements, and would
be in greater number. This they said with cunning,
to excite us to attack them by night, supposing that
we were ready; but they wished this because they had
dug ditches between their houses and the beach, and
they hoped that we should fall into them.

We however waited for daylight; we then leaped
into the water up to our thighs, for on account of the
shallow water and the rocks the boats could not come
close to the beach, and we had to cross two good cross-
bow shots through the water before reaching it. We
were forty-nine in number, the other eleven remained
in charge of the boats. When we reached land we
found the islanders fifteen hundred in number, drawn
up in three squadrons; they came down upon us with
terrible shouts, two squadrons attacking us on the
flanks, and the third in front. The captain then divided
his men in two bands. Our musketeers and crossbow-
men fired for half an hour from a distance, but did
nothing, since the bullets and arrows, though they
passed through their shields made of thin wood, and
perhaps wounded their arms, yet did not stop them.
The captain shouted not to fire, but he was not listened
to. The islanders seeing that the shots of our guns
did them little or no harm would not retire, but shouted
more loudly, and springing from one side to the other
to avoid our shots, they at the same time drew nearer

to us, throwing arrows, javelins, spears hardened in fire, stones, and even mud, so that we could hardly defend ourselves. Some of them cast lances pointed with iron at the captain-general.

He then, in order to disperse this multitude and to terrify them, sent some of our men to set fire to their houses, but this rendered them more ferocious. Some of them ran to the fire, which consumed twenty or thirty houses, and there killed two of our men. The rest came down upon us with greater fury; they perceived that our bodies were defended, but that the legs were exposed, and they aimed at them principally. The captain had his right leg pierced by a poisoned arrow, on which account he gave orders to retreat by degrees; but almost all our men took to precipitate flight, so that there remained hardly six or eight of us with him. We were oppressed by the lances and stones which the enemy hurled at us, and we could make no more resistance. The bombards which we had in the boats were of no assistance to us, for the shoal water kept them too far from the beach. We went thither, retreating little by little, and still fighting, and we had already got to the distance of a crossbow shot from the shore, having the water up to our knees, the islanders following and picking up again the spears which they had already cast, and they threw the same spear five or six times; as they knew the captain they aimed specially at him, and twice they knocked the helmet off his head. He, with a few of us, like a good knight, remained at his post without choosing to retreat further. Thus we fought for more than an hour, until an Indian succeeded in thrusting a cane lance into the captain's face. He then, being irritated, pierced the Indian's

breast with his lance, and left it in his body, and trying
to draw his sword he was unable to draw it more than
half way, on account of a javelin wound which he had
received in the right arm. The enemies seeing this all
rushed against him, and one of them with a great
sword, like a great scimitar gave him a great blow on
the left leg, which brought the captain down on his
face; then the Indians threw themselves upon him, and
ran him through with lances and scimitars, and all the
other arms which they had, so that they deprived of
life our mirror, light, comfort, and true guide. Whilst
the Indians were thus overpowering him, several times
he turned round towards us to see if we were all in safety,
as though his obstinate fight had no other object than
to give an opportunity for the retreat of his men. We
who fought to extremity, and who were covered with
wounds, seeing that he was dead, proceeded to the
boats which were on the point of going away. This
fatal battle was fought on the 27th of April of 1521, on
a Saturday; a day which the captain had chosen himself, because he had a special devotion to it. There
perished with him eight of our men, and four of the
Indians, who had become Christians; we had also many
wounded, amongst whom I must reckon myself. The
enemy lost only fifteen men.

He died; but I hope that your illustrious highness
will not allow his memory to be lost, so much the more
since I see revived in you the virtue of so great a
captain, since one of his principal virtues was constancy
in the most adverse fortune. In the midst of the sea
he was able to endure hunger better than we. Most
versed in nautical charts, he knew better than any
other the true art of navigation, of which it is a certain

proof that he knew by his genius, and his intrepidity, without any one having given him the example, how to attempt the circuit of the globe, which he had almost completed.

The Christian king could indeed have given us aid, and would have done so; but our captain far from foreseeing that which happened, when he landed with his men, had charged him not to come out of his balangai, wishing that he should stay there to see how we fought. When he knew how the captain had died he wept bitterly for him.

In the afternoon the king himself, with our consent, sent to tell the inhabitants of Matan, that if they would give up to us the body of our captain, and of our other companions who were killed in this battle, we would give them as much merchandise as they might wish for; but they answered that on no account would they ever give up that man, but they wished to preserve him as a monument of their triumph. When the death of the captain was known, those who were in the city to trade, had all the merchandise at once transported to the ships. We then elected in the place of the captain, Duarte Barbosa, a Portuguese, and a relation of the captain's, and Juan Serrano, a Spaniard.

Our interpreter, who was a slave of the captain-general, and was named Henry, having been slightly wounded in the battle, would not go ashore any more for the things which we required, but remained all day idle, and wrapped up in his mat (Schiavina). Duarte Barbosa, the commander of the flag ship, found fault with him, and told him that though his master was dead, he had not become free on that account, but that when we returned to Spain he would return him

to Doña Beatrice, the widow of the captain-general;
at the same time he threatened to have him flogged,
if he did not go on shore quickly, and do what was
wanted for the service of the ships. The slave rose up,
and did as though he did not care much for these affronts
and threats; and having gone on shore, he informed
the Christian king that we were thinking of going away
soon, but that if he would follow his advice, he might
become master of all our goods and of the ships themselves. The King of Zubu listened favourably to him,
and they arranged to betray us. After that the slave
returned on board, and showed more intelligence and
attention than he had done before.

Wednesday morning, the 1st of May, the Christian
king sent to tell the two commanders that the jewels
prepared as presents for the King of Spain were ready,
and he invited them to come that same day to dine
with him, with some of his most honoured companions,
and he would give them over to them. The commanders
went with twenty-four others, and amongst them was
our astrologer named San Martin of Seville. I could
not go because I was swelled with a wound from a
poisoned arrow in the forehead. Juan Carvalho, with
the chief of police, who also were invited, turned back,
and said that they had suspected some bad business,
because they had seen the man who had recovered
from illness by a miracle, leading away the priest to
his own house. They had hardly spoken these words
when we heard great lamentations and cries. We
quickly got up the anchors and, coming closer to
the beach, we fired several shots with the cannon
at the houses. There then appeared on the beach
Juan Serrano, in his shirt, wounded and bound, who

entreated us, as loudly as he could, not to fire any more, or else he would be massacred. We asked him what had become of his companions and the interpreter, and he said that all had been slain except the inter- preter. He then entreated us to ransom him with some merchandise; but Juan Carvalho, although he was his gossip, joined with some others, refused to do it, and they would not allow any boat to go ashore so that they might remain masters of the ships. Serrano continued his entreaties and lamentations, saying, that if we departed and abandoned him there, he would soon be killed; and after that he saw his lamentations were useless, he added that he prayed God to ask for an account of his life at the day of Judgment from Juan Carvalho, his gossip. Notwithstanding, we sailed immediately; and I never heard any more news of him.

In this island, before we lost our captain-general, we had news of Maluco.

When we were at a distance of eighteen leagues from the island of Zubu, near the head of another island called Bohol, in the midst of that archipelago, seeing that our crews were too much reduced in number, so that they were not sufficient for managing all the three ships, we burned the *Conception* after transporting into the other two all that it contained that was service- able. We then took the S.S.W. course, coasting along an island called Panilongon, where the people were black as in Ethiopia.

We then arrived at a large island, the king of which having come on board our ship, in order to show that he made alliance with us and would be friendly, drew blood from his left hand, and stained with it his breast.

his face, and the tip of his tongue. We then did likewise, and when the king went away, I alone accompanied him on shore to see the island.

We entered a river where we met many fishermen,
who presented some of their fish to the king. He then
took off the cloth which covered his middle, and some
of his chief men who were with him did the same : they
then all began to row and to sing. Passing near many
houses, which were on the brink of the river, we arrived
at two hours of the night at the house of the king, which
was two leagues from the mouth of the river where the
ships were.

When we reached the house, people came to meet us
with many torches, made of canes and palm leaves, full
of the before-mentioned gum, called *animé*. Whilst
supper was being got ready, the king, with two of his
chiefs, and two rather handsome ladies, drank a large
vase full of palm wine, without eating anything. I, ex-
cusing myself, saying that I had already supped, only
drank once. In drinking they use the ceremony which
I have already described in speaking of the King of
Mazzava. Then the supper was brought, which consisted of rice and fish, very much salted, in porcelain
dishes. Rice with them takes the place of bread.
They cook it in the following manner, which is common
to all these countries. They place inside an earthen
pot like ours, a large leaf which lines it all round
internally, then they put in the water and the rice,
and cover up the pot. They let it boil until the rice
has taken the consistency of bread, and then they take
it out in pieces.

When the supper was over the king had brought a
cane mat, and a mat of palm leaf, with a cushion of

leaves, and this was to be my bed. I slept there with one of his chiefs. The king with the two ladies went to sleep in another place.

When it was day, whilst breakfast was being prepared, I went to take a turn in the island, and entered several houses, constructed like those of the neighbouring islands; I saw there a good many utensils of gold, but very little victuals. I returned to the king's house, and we breakfasted with rice and fish. I succeeded in making the king understand by signs, that I should like to see the queen; and he made a sign to me that he was content, and we set out together to the top of a hill, under which her house was placed. I entered the house and made her an obeisance: she did likewise to me. I sat down by the side of her; she was weaving a palm mat to sleep upon. Throughout her house were seen porcelain vases suspended to the walls, and four metal timbals, of which one was very large, another of middle size, and two small ones, and she amused herself by playing on them. There were many male and female slaves for her service. We asked leave and returned to the king's house, who immediately ordered a refreshment of sugar canes.

On leaving this place, and taking our course between west and south-west, we touched at an almost uninhabited island, which afterwards we learned was named Cagayan. The few people there are Moors, who have been banished from an island called Burné. They go naked like the others, and carry blow-pipes with small quivers at their sides full of arrows, and a herb with which they poison them. They have daggers, with hilts adorned with gold and precious stones, lances, bucklers, and small cuirasses of buffaloes' hide. These

people took us for something Divine or holy. There
are some very large trees in this island, but little
victuals. It is in 7° 30′ North latitude, and forty-
three leagues from Chipit.

Continuing our voyage we changed our course to
between west and north-west, and after running
twenty-five leagues, we arrived at a large island,
which we found well provided with victuals, and it
was great good fortune for us, since we were so reduced
by hunger and so badly supplied, that we were several
times on the point of abandoning the ships, and estab-
lishing ourselves on some land, in order to live. In
this island, which we learned was named Palawan, we
found pigs, goats, fowls, yams, bananas of various
kinds, some of which are half a cubit long, and as
thick as the arm, others are only a span long, and
others are still smaller, and these are the best; they
have coco-nuts, sugar canes, and certain roots like
turnips. They cook rice under the fire in bamboo
canes, or wooden vessels, and it keeps longer than that
cooked in earthen pots. They draw from the rice with
a kind of alembic a wine that is better and stronger
than the palm wine. In short we found this island to
be a promised land.

Going from Palawan towards the south-west, after
a run of ten leagues, we reached another island. Whilst
coasting it, it seemed in a certain manner to go forward;
we coasted it for a distance of fully fifty leagues, until
we found a port. We had hardly reached the port
when the heavens were darkened, and the lights of
St Elmo appeared on our masts.

The next day the king of that island sent a prahu
to the ships; it was very handsome, with its prow and

stern ornamented with gold; on the bow fluttered a white and blue flag, with a tuft of peacock's feathers at the top of the staff; there were in the prahu some people playing on pipes and drums, and many other persons. Two almadias followed the prahu; these are fishermen's boats, and a prahu is a kind of fusta. Eight old men of the chiefs of the island came into the ships, and sat down upon a carpet on the poop, and presented a painted wooden vase full of betel and areca (fruits which they constantly chew), with orange and jessamine flowers, and covered over with a cloth of yellow silk. They also gave two cages full of fowls, two goats, three vessels full of wine, distilled from rice, and some bundles of sugar cane. They did the same to the other ship; and embracing us they departed. Their rice wine is clear like water, but so strong that many of our men were intoxicated. They call it arrack.

Six days later the king again sent three very ornamented prahus, which came playing pipes and drums and cymbals, and going round the ships, their crews saluted us with their cloth caps, which hardly cover the tops of their heads. We saluted them, firing the bombards without stones. Then they made us a present of various victuals, but all made with rice, either wrapped in leaves in the form of a long cylinder, or in the shape of a sugar loaf, or in the shape of a cake, with eggs and honey. They then said that their king was well pleased that we should make provisions here of wood and water, and that we might traffic at our pleasure with the islanders. Having heard this, seven of us entered one of the prahus, taking with us presents for the king, and for some of his court. The present intended for the king consisted in a Turkish coat of green velvet, a chair of violet coloured velvet, five ells of red cloth, a cap, a gilt goblet, and a vase of glass, with its cover, three packets of paper, and a gilt pen and ink case. We took for the queen three ells of yellow cloth, a pair of slippers, ornamented with silver, and a silver case full of pins. For the king's governor or minister three ells of red cloth, a cap, and a gilt goblet; and for the herald who had come in the prahu, a coat of the Turkish fashion, of red and green colours, a cap and a packet of paper. For the other seven chief men who had come with him, we prepared presents; for one cloth, for another a cap, and for each a packet of paper. Having made these preparations, we entered the prahu, and departed.

When we arrived at the city, we were obliged to wait about two hours in the prahu, until there came thither two elephants covered with silk, and twelve men, each of whom carried a porcelain vase covered with silk, for conveying and wrapping up our presents. We mounted the elephants, and those twelve men preceded us, carrying the vases with our presents. We went as far as the house of the governor, who gave us supper with many sorts of viands. There we slept through the night, on mattresses filled with cotton, and covered with silk, with sheets of Cambay stuff.

On the following day we remained doing nothing in the house till midday, and after that we set out for the king's palace. We were again mounted upon the elephants, and the men with the presents preceded us as before. From the governor's house to that of the king, all the streets were full of men armed with swords, spears, and bucklers, the king having so commanded. We entered the palace still mounted upon the elephants;

we then dismounted, and ascended a staircase, accompanied by the governor and some of the chief men, and entered a large room full of courtiers, whom we should call the barons of the kingdom; there we sat upon a carpet, and the vases with the presents were placed near us.

At the end of this hall there was another a little higher, but not so large, all hung with silk stuffs, among which were two curtains of brocade hung up, and leaving open two windows which gave light to the room.

There were placed three hundred men of the king's guard with naked daggers in their hands, which they held on their thighs. At the end of this second hall was a great opening, covered with a curtain of brocade, and on this being raised we saw the king sitting at a table, with a little child of his, chewing betel. Behind him there were only women.

Then one of the chief men informed us that we could not speak to the king, but that if we wished to convey anything to him, we were to say it to him, and he would say it to a chief or courtier of higher rank, who would lay it before a brother of the governor, who was in the smaller room, and they by means of a blow pipe placed in a fissure in the wall would communicate our thoughts to a man who was near the king, and from him the king would understand them. He taught us meanwhile to make three obeisances to the king, with the hands joined above the head, raising first one then the other foot, and then to kiss the hands to him. This is the royal obeisance.

Then by the mode which had been indicated to us, we gave him to understand that we belonged to the

King of Spain, who wished to be in peace with him, and wished for nothing else than to be able to trade with his island. The king caused an answer to be given that he was most pleased that the King of Spain was his friend, and that we could take wood and water in his states, and traffic according to our pleasure. That done we offered the presents, and at each thing which they gave to him, he made a slight inclination with his head. To each of us was then given some brocade, with cloth of gold, and some silk, which they placed upon one of our shoulders, and then took away to take care of them. A collation of cloves and cinnamon was then served to us, and after that the curtains were drawn and the windows closed. All the men who were in the palace had their middles covered with cloth of gold and silk, they carried in their hands daggers with gold hilts, adorned with pearls and precious stones, and they had many rings on their fingers.

We again mounted the elephants, and returned to the house of the governor. Seven men preceded us there, carrying the presents made to us, and when we reached the house they gave to each one of us what was for him, putting it on our left shoulder, as had been done in the king's palace. To each of these seven men we gave a pair of knives in recompense for their trouble.

Afterwards there came nine men to the governor's house, sent by the king, with as many large wooden trays, in each of which were ten or twelve china dishes, with the flesh of various animals, such as veal, capons, fowls, peacocks, and others, with various sorts of fish, so that only of flesh there were thirty or thirty-two different viands. We supped on the ground on a palm mat; at each mouthful we drank a little china cup of the size of an egg full of the distilled liquor of rice: we then ate some rice and some things made of sugar, using gold spoons made like ours. In the place in which we passed the two nights there were two candles of white wax always burning, placed on high chandeliers of silver, and two oil lamps with four wicks each. Two men kept watch there to take care of them. The next morning we came upon the same elephants to the sea shore, where there were two prahus ready, in which we were taken back to the ships.

This city is entirely built on foundations in the salt water, except the houses of the king and some of the princes: it contains twenty-five thousand fires or families. The houses are all of wood, placed on great piles to raise them high up. When the tide rises the women go in boats through the city selling provisions and necessaries. In front of the king's house there is a wall made of great bricks, with barbicans like forts, upon which were fifty-six bombards of metal, and six of iron. They fired many shots from them during the two days that we passed in the city.

The king to whom we presented ourselves is a Moor, and is named Raja Siripada: he is about forty years of age, and is rather corpulent. No one serves him except ladies who are the daughters of the chiefs. No one speaks to him except by means of the blow-pipe as has been described above. He has ten scribes, who write down his affairs on thin bark of trees, and are called *chiritoles*. He never goes out of his house except to go hunting.

On Monday, the 29th of July, we saw coming towards us more than a hundred prahus, divided into three squadrons, and as many *tungulis*, which are their smaller kind of boats. At this sight, and fearing treachery, we hurriedly set sail, and left behind an anchor in the sea.

On leaving this island we returned backwards to look for a convenient place for caulking our ships, which were leaking, and one of them, through the negligence of the pilot, struck on a shoal near an island named Bibalon; but, by the help of God, we got her off. We also ran another great danger, for a sailor, in snuffing a candle, threw the lighted wick into a chest of gunpowder; but he was so quick in picking it out that the powder did not catch fire.

On our way we saw four prahus. We took one laden with coco-nuts on its way to Burné; but the crew escaped to a small island, and the other three prahus escaped behind some other small islands.

Between the northern cape of Burné and the island named Cimbonbon, situated in 8° 7′ N. latitude there is a very convenient port for refitting ships, and we entered it; but as we were wanting many things necessary for our work, we had to spend there forty-two days. Each one worked at one thing or another according to the best of his knowledge or ability; but our greatest labour was going to get wood in the thickets, as the ground was covered with briars and thorny shrubs, and we had no shoes.

Saturday, the 26th of October, about nightfall, whilst coasting the island of Birabam Batolac, we met with a very great storm, before which we lowered all our sails, and betook ourselves to prayer. Then our three saints appeared upon the masts and dispersed the darkness. St Elmo stood for more than two hours at the mainmast head like a flame. St Nicholas at the head of the foremast, and St Clara on the mizenmast. In gratitude for their assistance we promised a slave to each of the saints, and we gave to each an offering.

Continuing our voyage we entered a port between the two islands Sarangani and Candigar, and cast anchor to the east, near a village of Sarangani, where pearls and gold are found. This port is in 5° 9' N. latitude, and fifty leagues from Cavit. The inhabitants are Gentiles and go naked like the others.

Having remained here a day we compelled by force two pilots to come with us to show us the way to Maluco. We were directed to take a south-south-west course, and passed between eight islands partly inhabited, partly uninhabited, which formed a kind of street. These were named Cheava, Caviao, Cabiao, Camanuca, Cabaluzao, Cheai, Lipan, and Nuza. At the end of these we reached an island which was very beautiful, named Sanghir. But having a contrary wind, which did not allow us to double the cape, we tacked about backwards and forwards near it.

On this occasion, profiting by the darkness of the night, one of the pilots whom we had caught at Sarangani, escaped by swimming and reached that island.

Wednesday, the 6th of November, we discovered four other rather high islands at a distance of fourteen leagues towards the east. The pilot who had remained with us told us those were the Maluco islands, for which we gave thanks to God, and to comfort ourselves we discharged all our artillery. It need not cause wonder that we were so much rejoiced, since we had passed twenty-seven months less two days always in search of Maluco, wandering for that object among the immense number of islands. But I must say that near all these islands the least depth that we found was one hundred fathoms, for which reason attention is not to be given to all that the Portuguese have spread, according to whom the islands of Maluco are situated in seas which cannot be navigated on account of the shoals, and the dark and foggy atmosphere.

Friday, the 8th November of 1521, three hours before sunset, we entered a port of the island called Tadore, and having gone near the shore, we cast anchor in twenty fathoms, and discharged all our artillery. Next day the king came to the ships in a prahu, and went round them. We went to meet him with a boat to show him honour, and he made us enter his prahu, and sit near him. He was sitting under a silk umbrella, which sheltered him. In front of him was his son with the royal sceptre, there were also two men with gold vases to give him water for his hands, and two others with gilt caskets full of betel.

The king gave us a welcome, and said that a long time back he had dreamed that some ships were coming to Maluco from distant countries, and that to assure himself with respect to this, he had examined the moon, and he had seen that they were really coming, and that indeed they were our ships. After that he came on board our ships, and we all kissed his hand: we then conducted him to the poop, but he, in order to avoid stooping, would not enter the cabin except by the upper opening. We made him sit down on a chair of red velvet, and placed on him a Turkish robe of yellow velvet. In order to do him more honour we sat down before him on the ground. When he had heard who we were, and what was the object of our voyage, he

said that he and all his people were well content to be the
most faithful friends and vassals of the King of Spain;
that he received us in this island as his own sons; that
we might go on shore and remain there as in our own
houses; and that his island for the future should not
be named Tadore, but Castile, in proof of the great love
he bore to the king our master. Then we presented to
him the chair on which he sat, and the robe which we
had put on him, a piece of fine linen, four ells of scarlet
cloth, a robe of brocade, a cloth of yellow damask, a
piece of the whitest Cambay linen, two caps, six strings
of glass beads, twelve knives, three large mirrors, six
scissors, six combs, some gilt goblets, and other things.
We gave to his son an Indian cloth of gold and silk,
a large mirror, a cap and two knives. To each of the
nine chief men of his suite we made a present of a piece
of silk, a cap and two knives; and to many others of
his suite we made a present, to one of a cap, to another
of a knife, until the king told us not to give any more
presents. He then said that he had got nothing worthy
to be sent as a present to our king, unless he sent
himself, now that he considered him as his lord. He
invited us to come closer to the city, and if any one
attempted to come on board the ships at night, he told
us to fire upon him with our guns. He came out of the
stern cabin by the same way by which he had entered
it, without ever bending his head. At his departure we
fired all the cannon.

This king is a Moor, of about forty-five years of age,
rather well made, and of a handsome presence. He is a
very great astrologer. His dress consisted of a shirt of
very fine white stuff, with the ends of the sleeves embroidered with gold, and a wrapper which came down

from his waist almost to the ground. He was bare-footed; round his head he had a silk veil, and over that a garland of flowers. He is named Raja Sultan Manzor.

On the 10th of November—a Sunday—we had another conversation with the king, who wished to know how long a time we had been absent from Spain, and what pay and what rations the king gave to each of us; and we told him all this. He asked us for a signature of the king and a royal standard, since he desired that both his island of Tadore, and also that of Tarenate (where he intended to have his nephew named Calanogapi, crowned king) should become subject to the King of Spain, for whose honour he would fight to the death; and if it should happen that he should be compelled to give way, he would take refuge in Spain with all his family, in a new junk which he was having constructed, and would take with him the royal signature and standard.

He begged us to leave with him some of our men, who would always keep alive his recollection of us and of our king, as he would more esteem having some of us with him than our merchandise, which would not last him a long time. Seeing our eagerness to take cloves on board, he said that for that purpose he would go to an island called Bachian, where he hoped to find as much of them as were wanted, since in his island there was not a quantity sufficient of dry cloves to load the two ships. On that day there was no traffic because it was Sunday. The holiday of these people is on Friday.

It may please your illustrious lordship to have some description of the islands where the cloves grow. They are five—Tarenate, Tadore, Mutir, Machian, and

Bachian. Tarenate is the principal island. Its king, whilst he lived, had almost entire dominion over the other four. Tadore, the island in which we were, has its own king. Mutir and Machian have no king, but are governed by the people; and when the kings of Tarenate and Tadore are at war, they furnish them with combatants. The last is Bachian, and it has a king. All this province in which the cloves grow is called Maluco.

When we arrived here, eight months had not elapsed since a certain Portuguese, Francisco Serrano, had died in Tarènate.

Francisco Serrano was a great friend and a relation of our unfortunate captain-general, and he it was who induced him to undertake that voyage, for when Magellan was at Malacca, he had several times learned by letters from Serrano that he was here. Therefore, when D. Manuel, King of Portugal, refused to increase his pension by a single testoon per month, an increase which he thought he had well deserved, he came to Spain and made the proposal to his Sacred Majesty to come here by way of the west, and he obtained all that he asked for.

Every day there came to the ships many boats laden with goats, fowls, plantains, coco-nuts, and other victuals, that it was a wonder to see. We supplied the ships with good water taken from a spring whence it issued hot, but if it remains only one hour in the open air it becomes very cold. They say that it comes out like that because it issues from the mountain of the cloves. It may be seen from this how those lied who said that fresh water had to be brought to Maluco from distant countries.

The next day the king sent his son named Mossahap to the island of the Mutir for cloves with which to freight our ships.

In the evening of the same day Pedro Alfonso, the Portuguese, came in a prahu, but before he came on board the ships the king sent to call him, and said to him, that although he belonged to Tarenate he should take good care not to answer falsely to the questions we were going to ask him. He indeed, after coming on board, told us that he had come to India sixteen years ago, and of these years he had passed ten in Maluco; and it was just ten years since those islands had been discovered by the Portuguese, who kept the discovery secret from us.

Friday, the 15th of November, the king told us that he thought of going himself to Bachian to get the cloves which the Portuguese had left there, and asked us for presents to give to the two governors of Mutir in the name of the King of Spain. Meanwhile, having come close to our ships, he wished to see how we shot with the cross-bow, with guns, and with a swivel gun, which is a weapon larger than an arquebuse. He himself fired three times with a cross-bow, but he did not care to fire with a gun.

Opposite Tadore there is another very large island, called Gilolo, and it is so large that a prahu can with difficulty go round it in four months.

Sunday morning I went on shore to see how the cloves grow, and this is what I observed. The tree from which they are gathered is high, and its trunk is as thick as a man's body, more or less, according to the age of the plant. Its branches spread out somewhat in the middle of the tree, but near the top they form a pyramid. The bark is of an olive colour, and the leaves very like those of the laurel. The cloves grow at the end of little branches in bunches of ten or twenty. These trees always bear more fruit on one side than on the other, according to the seasons. The cloves are white when they first sprout, they get red as they ripen, and blacken when dry. They are gathered twice in the year, once about Christmas and the other time about St John's day, when the air in these countries is milder, and it is still more so in December. When the year is rather hot, and there is little rain, they gather in each of these islands from three to four hundred bahars of cloves. The clove tree does not live except in the mountains, and if it is transferred to the plain it dies there. The leaf, the bark, and the wood, as long as they are green, have the strength and fragrance of the fruit itself. If these are not gathered when just ripe they get so large and hard that nothing of them remains good except the rind. It is said that the mist renders them perfect, and indeed we saw almost every day a mist descend and surround one or other of the above-mentioned mountains. Among these people everyone possesses some of these trees, and each man watches over his own trees and gathers their fruit, but does not do any work round them to cultivate them. This tree does not grow except in the five mountains of the five Maluco islands. There are, however, a few trees in Gilolo and in a small island between Tadore and Mutir named Mare, but they are not good.

There are in this island of Gilolo some trees of nutmegs. These are like our walnuts, and the leaves also are similar. The nutmeg, when gathered, is like the quince in form and colour, and the down which covers it, but it is smaller. The outside rind is as thick as the green rind of our walnuts, beneath which is a thin web, or rather cartilage, under which is the mace, of a very bright red, which covers and surrounds the rind of the nuts, inside which is the nutmeg properly so called.

There also grows in Tadore the ginger, which we used to eat green, instead of bread. Ginger is not a tree, but a shrub, which sends out of the earth shoots a span long like the shoots of canes, which they also resemble in the shape of the leaves, only those of the ginger are narrower. The shoots are good for nothing; that which makes ginger is the root. When green, it is not so strong as when it is dry, and to dry it they use lime, or else it would not keep.

Every day there came from Tarenate many boats laden with cloves, but we, because we were waiting for the king, would not traffic for those goods, but only for victuals: and the men of Tarenate complained much of this.

On Sunday night, the 24th of November, the king arrived, and on entering the port had his drums sounded, and passed between our ships. We fired many bombards to do him honour. He told us that for four days we should be continually supplied with cloves.

In effect, on Monday he sent seven hundred and ninety one catils, without taking tare. To take tare means to take spice for less than what it weighs, and the reason of this is because when they are fresh, every day they diminish in weight. As these were the first cloves which we took on board, and the principal object of our voyage, we fired our bombards for joy. Cloves are called *Gomode* in this place; in Sarangani where we took the two pilots they are called *Bonglavan*, and in Malacca *Chianche*.

Tuesday the 26th November the King came to tell us that for us he had done what a King never does here, that was to leave his own island; but he had gone to show the affection he had for the King of Castile, and because when we had got our cargo, we could sooner return to Spain, and afterwards return with greater forces to avenge the death of his father, who had been killed in an island called Buru, and his body had been thrown into the sea.

He afterwards added that it was the custom in Tadore, when the first cloves were embarked in a vessel, or in junks, that the king gave a feast to their crews and merchants, and they made prayers to God to bring them in safety to their port. He wished to do the same for us, and at the same time the feast would serve for the King of Bachian, who was coming with a brother of his to pay him a visit, and on that account he had the streets cleaned. Hearing this, some of us began to suspect some treachery; all the more because we learned that, not long before, three Portuguese of the companions of Francisco Serrano had been assassinated at the place where we got water, by some of the islanders concealed in the thickets; also we often saw them whispering with the Indians whom we had made prisoners. Therefore, although some of us were inclined to accept the invitation, we concluded not to betake ourselves thither, recollecting the unfortunate feast given to our men in the island of Zubu, and we decided on a speedy departure.

Meantime a message was sent to the king to thank
him, and to ask him to come soon to the ships, where we
would deliver to him the four men we had promised
him, with the goods which we had destined for him.
The King came soon, and on entering the ship, as
though he had observed that we had doubts, said that
he entered with as much confidence and security as
into his own house. He made us feel how much he
was displeased by our unexpected haste to depart,
since ships used to employ thirty days in taking in
their cargo; and that if he had made a journey out
of the island, he certainly had not done it to injure us
but to assist us, so that we might more speedily obtain
the cloves which we required, and a part of which we
were still expecting. He added that it was not then
a fit season for navigating in those seas, on account of
the many shoals near Bandan, and besides it would be
a likely thing that we should fall in with some Portuguese ships. When, in spite of what he had said, he
saw we were still determined on going away, he said
that we must take back all that we had given him,
since the Kings, his neighbours, would consider him
as a man without reputation for receiving so many
presents in the name of so great a king as the King
of Spain, and he had given nothing in return, and
perhaps they would suspect that the Spaniards had
gone away in such haste for fear of some treachery,
so that they would fix upon him the name of traitor.
Then, in order that no suspicion might remain in our
minds of his honesty and good faith, he ordered his
Koran to be brought, and kissing it devoutly he placed
it four or five times on his head whilst whispering
certain words to himself, with a rite which they call

Zambehan, and he said in the presence of us all, that he swore by Allah and by the Koran, which he held in his hand, that he would ever be faithful and a friend to the King of Spain. He said all this almost weeping and with so great an appearance of sincerity and cordiality, that we promised to prolong our sojourn at Tadore for another fortnight. We then gave him the Royal signature and standard. We learned later, by a sure and certain channel, that some of the chiefs of those islands had indeed counselled him to kill all of us, by which thing he would have acquired for himself great merit with the Portuguese, who would have given him good assistance to avenge himself on the King of Bachian, but he, loyal and constant to the King of Spain, with whom he had sworn a peace, had answered that he would never do such an act on any account whatever.

Wednesday, the 27th November, the king issued a proclamation that whoever had cloves might freely sell them to us. For which reason all that and the following day, we bought cloves like mad.

Friday, in the afternoon, the governor of Machian came with many prahus, but he would not come on shore, because his father and his brother, who had been banished from Machian, had taken refuge here.

The following day the King of Tadore, with his nephew, the governor, named Humai, a man of twenty-five years of age, came on board the ships, and the king, on hearing that we had no more cloth, sent to fetch from his house six ells of red cloth, and gave them to us in order that we might, by adding other objects, make a fitting present to the governor. We made him the present, and he thanked us much, and said that soon he would send us plenty of cloves. At his departure from the ship we fired several bombards.

Sunday the 1st day of December, the above-mentioned governor departed from Tadore; and we were told that the king had made him a present of some silk cloths and drums, for him to send us the cloves sooner. On Monday, the king himself went again out of the island for the same object. Wednesday morning, as it was the day of St Barbara, and on account of the King's arrival all the artillery was discharged. The king came to the beach to see how we fired rockets and fire balls, and took great pleasure in them.

Thursday and Friday we purchased a good many cloves both in the city and at the ships at a much lower price, as the time of our departure grew nearer. For four ells of ribbon they gave a bahar of cloves, for two little chains of brass which were worth a marcello, they gave us a hundred pounds; and at last each man being desirous of having his portion of the cargo, and as there were no more goods to give in exchange for cloves, one gave his cloak, another his coat, and another a shirt or other clothes to obtain them.

The king had informed us that the King of Bachian would soon arrive, with a brother of his who was going to marry one of his daughters, and had asked us to do him honour by firing bombards on his arrival. He arrived on Sunday the 15th of December, in the afternoon, and we did him honour as the king had desired; we did not, however, discharge the heavier cannon, as we were heavily laden. The king and his brother came in a prahu with three banks of rowers on each side, a hundred and twenty in number. The prahu was adorned with many streamers made of white, yellow and red parrot's feathers. They were sounding many cymbals, and that sound served to give the measure to the rowers to keep time. In two other prahus were the damsels who were to be presented to the bride. They returned us the salute by going round the ships and round the port.

As it is the custom that no king disembarks on the land of another king, the King of Tadore came to visit him of Bachian in his own prahu: this one, seeing the other coming, rose from the carpet on which he was sitting, and placed himself on one side to make way for the king of the country: but he, out of ceremony, would not sit on the carpet, but sat on the other side of it, leaving the carpet between them. Then the King of Bachian gave to him of Tadore five hundred *patol*, as if in payment of the daughter he was giving as a wife to his brother. *Patols* are cloths of gold and silk worked in China, and are very much prized in these islands. Each of these cloths is paid for with three bahars of cloves more or less, according as they are more or less rich in gold and embroidery. Whenever one of the chief men die, his relations put on these cloths to do him honour.

Monday, the King of Tadore sent a dinner to the King of Bachian, carried by fifty women clothed with silk from their waists to their knees. They went two and two with a man between in the midst of them. Each one carried a large dish upon which were small dishes with various viands; ten of the oldest of these women were the mace-bearers. They proceeded in this way to the prahu, and presented everything to the king who was sitting on a carpet under a red and yellow canopy. As they were returning, they caught

some of our men who had come out of curiosity and
who were obliged to make them presents of some trifle
to get free. After that the king sent also to us a
present of goats, coco-nuts, wine, and other things.

This day we bent on the ships new sails, upon which
was the cross of St James, of Galicia, with letters
which said: "This is the figure of our good fortune."

Tuesday, we presented to the king some pieces of
artillery; that is some arquebuses which we had taken
as prizes in the Indies, and some of our swivel-guns
with four barrels of powder. We took on board each
ship eighty barrels of water. Wood we were to find
at the island of Mare, where the king had already five
days ago sent a hundred men to prepare it, and near
which we were to pass.

This day, the King of Bachian, with the consent of
the King of Tadore, came on shore, preceded by four
men holding up daggers in their hands, to make alliance
with us: he said, in the presence of the King of Tadore
and of all his suite, that he would always be ready for
the service of the King of Spain, that he would keep in
his name the cloves left in his island by the Portuguese,
until another Spanish squadron arrived there, and he
would not give them up without his consent. He sent
through us to the King of Spain a present of a slave
and two bahars of cloves. He would have wished to
have sent ten bahars, but our ships were so heavily
laden, that we could not receive any more.

He also gave us for the King of Spain two most
beautiful dead birds. These birds are as large as
thrushes; they have small heads, long beaks, legs
slender like a writing pen, and a span in length;
they have no wings, but instead of them long feathers

of different colours, like plumes: their tail is like that of the thrush. All the feathers, except those of the wings, are of a dark colour; they never fly, except when the wind blows. They told us that these birds come from the terrestrial Paradise, and they call them "bolon divata," that is divine birds.

One day the King of Tadore sent to tell our men, who dwelt in the magazine for the merchandise, that they should take care not to go out of the house by night, since there were certain men, natives of the country, who by anointing themselves, walk by night in the shape of men without heads: and if they meet anyone to whom they wish ill, they touch his hand and anoint his palm, and that ointment causes him soon to grow ill, and die at the end of three or four days. But if they meet three or four persons together they do not touch them, but make them giddy. He added that he had a watch kept to discover them, and he had already had several executed.

When they build a new house, before going to inhabit it, they make a fire round it, and give many feasts there. Then they fasten to the roof of the house a pattern or sample of everything that is to be found in the island, persuaded that by that means none of those things will be ever wanting to whoever inhabits the house.

Wednesday morning everything was prepared for our departure from Maluco. The Kings of Tadore, of Gilolo, and of Bachian, and a son of the King of Tarenate had come to accompany us as far as the island of Mare. The ship *Victoria* made sail and stood out a little, waiting for the ship *Trinity*; but she had much difficulty in getting up the anchor, and meanwhile the sailors perceived that she was leaking very much in the hold. Then the *Victoria* returned to anchor in her former position. They began to discharge the cargo of the *Trinity* to see if the leak could be stopped, for it was perceived that the water came in with force as through a pipe, but we were never able to find out at what part it came in. All that day and the next we did nothing else but work at the pumps, but without any advantage.

Hearing this, the King of Tadore came at once to the ships, and occupied himself with us in searching for the leak. For this purpose he sent into the sea five of his men, who were accustomed to remain a long time under the water, and although they remained more than half-an-hour they could not find the fissure. As the water inside the ship continually increased, the king, who was as much affected by it as we were, and lamenting this misfortune, sent to the end of the island for three other men, more skilful than the first at remaining under water.

He came with them early the next morning. These men dived under water with their hair loose, thinking that their hair, attracted by the water which penetrated into the ship, would indicate to them the leak, but though they remained more than an hour in the water, they did not find it. The king, seeing that there was no remedy for it, said with lamentation, "Who will go to Spain to take news of me to the king our lord?" We answered him that the *Victoria* would go there, and would sail at once to take advantage of the east winds, which had already commenced. The *Trinity* meanwhile, would be refitted and would wait for the west winds and go to Darien, which is on the other side of the sea, in the country of Diucatan. The king approved our thoughts, and said that he had in his service two hundred and twenty-five carpenters who would do all the work under the direction of our men, and that those who should remain there would be treated as his own children, and he said this with so much emotion that he moved us all to tears.

We, who were on board the *Victoria*, fearing that she might open, on account of the heavy cargo and the long voyage, lightened her by discharging sixty hundred weight of cloves, which we had carried to the house where the crew of the *Trinity* were lodged. Some of our own crew preferred to remain at Maluco rather than go with us to Spain, because they feared that the ship could not endure so long a voyage, and because, mindful of how much they had suffered, they feared to die of hunger in mid-ocean.

Saturday, the 21st December, day of St Thomas the Apostle, the King of Tadore came to the ships and brought us the two pilots, whom we had already paid, to conduct us out of these islands. They said that the weather was then good for sailing at once, but, having to wait for the letters of our companions who remained behind, and who wished to write to Spain, we could not sail till midday. Then the ships took leave of one another by a mutual discharge of bombards. Our men accompanied us for some distance with their boat, and then with tears and embraces we separated. Juan Carvalho remained at Tadore with fifty-three of our men: we were forty-seven Europeans and thirteen Indians.

The king's governor came with us as far as the island of Mare: we had hardly arrived there when

four prahus laden with wood came up, which in less
than an hour we got on board. We then took the
south-west course.

[After leaving Mare, their course took them past
the Xulla islands, Buru, Mallua—now Ombay—where
they spent fifteen days in caulking their ship, and
Timor, where they arrived towards the end of January
1522. After coasting the north-west side of this island,
they sailed about the middle of February S.S.W. across
the Indian Ocean.]

In order to double the Cape of Good Hope, we went as
far as 42° South latitude, and we remained off that cape
for nine weeks, with the sails struck on account of the
Western and North-western gales which beat against
our bows with fierce squalls. The Cape of Good Hope
is in 34° 30′ South latitude, 1600 leagues distant from
the Cape of Malacca, and it is the largest and most
dangerous cape in the world.

Some of our men, and among them the sick, would
have liked to land at a place belonging to the Portuguese
called Mozambique, both because the ship made much
water, and because of the great cold which we suffered;
and much more because we had nothing but rice and
water for food and drink, all the meat of which we had
made provision having putrefied, for the want of salt
had not permitted us to salt it. But the greater
number of us, prizing honour more than life itself,
decided on attempting at any risk to return to Spain.

At length, by the aid of God, on the 6th of May, we
passed that terrible cape, but we were obliged to
approach it within only five leagues distance, or else
we should never have passed it. We then sailed
towards the north-west for two whole months without

ever taking rest; and in this short time we lost twenty-
one men between Christians and Indians. We made
then a curious observation on throwing them into the
sea, that was that the Christians remained with the
face turned to the sky, and the Indians with the face
turned to the sea. If God had not granted us favourable weather, we should all have perished of hunger.

Constrained by extreme necessity, we decided on
touching at the Cape Verde Islands, and on Wednesday
the 9th of July, we touched at one of those islands
named St James's. Knowing that we were in an
enemy's country, and amongst suspicious persons, on
sending the boat ashore to get provision of victuals,
we charged the seamen to say to the Portuguese that
we had sprung our foremast under the equinoctial line
(although this misfortune had happened at the Cape of
Good Hope), and that our ship was alone, because
whilst we tried to repair it, our captain-general had
gone with the other two ships to Spain. With these
good words, and giving some of our merchandise in
exchange, we obtained two boat-loads of rice.

In order to see whether we had kept an exact account
of the days, we charged those who went ashore to ask
what day of the week it was, and they were told by the
Portuguese inhabitants of the island that it was Thursday, which was a great cause of wondering to us, since
with us it was only Wednesday. We could not persuade
ourselves that we were mistaken; and I was more sur-
prised than the others, since having always been in good
health, I had every day, without intermission, written
down the day that was current. But we were afterwards advised that there was no error on our part,
since as we had always sailed towards the west, following

the course of the sun, and had returned to the same place, we must have gained twenty-four hours, as is clear to any one who reflects upon it.

The boat, having returned for rice a second time to the shore, was detained, with thirteen men who were in it. As we saw that, and, from the movement in certain caravels, suspected that they might wish to capture us and our ship, we at once set sail. We afterwards learned, some time after our return, that our boat and men had been arrested, because one of our men had discovered the deception, and said that the captain-general was dead, and that our ship was the only one remaining of Magellan's fleet.

At last, when it pleased Heaven, on Saturday the 6th of September of the year 1522, we entered the bay of San Lucar; and of sixty men who composed our crew when we left Maluco, we were reduced to only eighteen, and these for the most part sick. Of the others, some died of hunger, some had run away at the island of Timor, and some had been condemned to death for their crimes.

From the day when we left this bay of San Lucar until our return thither, we reckoned that we had run more than fourteen thousand four hundred and sixty leagues, and we had completed going round the earth from East to West.

Monday the 8th of September, we cast anchor near the mole of Seville, and discharged all the artillery.

Tuesday, we all went in shirts and barefoot, with a taper in our hands to visit the shrine of St Maria of Victory, and of St Maria de Antigua.

DRAKE'S FAMOUS VOYAGE (1577—1580)

By Francis Pretty

The famous voyage of Sir Francis Drake into the South
   Sea, and therehence about the whole Globe of the
   earth, begun in the year of our Lord, 1577.

The 15 day of November, in the year of our Lord
1577, Master Francis Drake, with a fleet of five ships
and barks, and to the number of 164 men, gentlemen
and sailors, departed from Plymouth, giving out his
pretended voyage for Alexandria: but the wind falling
contrary, he was forced the next morning to put into
Falmouth haven in Cornwall, where such and so terrible
a tempest took us, as few men have seen the like, and
was indeed so vehement, that all our ships were like
to have gone to wreck. But it pleased God to preserve
us from that extremity, and to afflict us only for that
present with these two particulars: the mast of our
Admiral, which was the *Pelican*, was cut overboard for
the safeguard of the ship, and the *Marigold* was driven
ashore, and somewhat bruised. For the repairing of
which damages we returned again to Plymouth, and
having recovered those harms, and brought the ships
again to good state, we set forth the second time from
Plymouth, and set sail the 13 day of December following.

Sir Francis Drake

The 25 day of the same month we fell with the Cape Cantin, upon the coast of Barbary, and coasting along, the 27 day we found an island called Mogador, lying one mile distant from the main, between which island and the main, we found a very good and safe harbour for our ships to ride in, as also very good entrance, and void of any danger.

On this island our General erected a pinnace, whereof he brought out of England with him four already framed. While these things were in doing, there came to the water's side some of the inhabitants of the country, showing forth their flags of truce, which being seen of our General, he sent his ship's boat to the shore, to know what they would. They being willing to come aboard, our men left there one man of our company for a pledge, and brought two of theirs aboard our ship, which by signs showed our General, that the next day they would bring some provision, as sheep, capons and hens, and such like: whereupon our General bestowed amongst them some linen cloth and shoes, and a javelin, which they very joyfully received, and departed for that time.

The next morning they failed not to come again to the water's side, and our General again setting out our boat, one of our men leaping over-rashly ashore, and offering friendly to embrace them, they set violent hands on him, offering a dagger to his throat if he had made any resistance, and so laying him on a horse, carried him away. So that a man cannot be too circumspect and wary of himself among such miscreants.

Our pinnace being finished, we departed from this place the 30 and last day of December, and coasting along the shore, we did descry, not contrary to our

expectation, certain canters, which were Spanish fishermen; to whom we gave chase and took three of them,
and proceeding further we met with 3 caravels and took
them also.

The 17 day of January we arrived at Cape Blanco,
where we found a ship riding at anchor, within the
Cape, and but two simple mariners in her.   Which ship
we took and carried her further into the harbour, where
we remained 4 days, and in that space our General
mustered and trained his men on land in warlike
manner, to make them fit for all occasions.

In this place we took of the fishermen such necessaries as we wanted, and they could yield us, and
leaving here one of our little barks called the *Benedict*,
we took with us one of theirs which they called canters,
being of the burden of 40 tons or thereabouts.

All these things being finished, we departed this
harbour the 22 of January, carrying along with us
one of the Portugal caravels which was bound to the
Islands of Cape Verde for salt, whereof good store is
made in one of those islands.

The master or pilot of that caravel did advertise our
General that upon one of those islands called Mayo,
there was great store of dried cabritos, which a few
inhabitants there dwelling did yearly make ready for
such of the king's ships as did there touch, being bound
for his country of Brazil or elsewhere.   We fell with
this island the 27 of January, but the inhabitants
would in no case traffic with us, being thereof forbidden
by the king's edict: yet the next day our General sent
to view the island, and the likelihoods that might be
there of provision of victuals, about threescore and two
men under the conduct and government of Master

Winter and Master Doughty, and marching towards the chief place of habitation in this island (as by the Portugal we were informed), having travelled to the mountains the space of three miles, and arriving there somewhat before the daybreak, we arrested ourselves to see day before us. Which appearing, we found the inhabitants to be fled: but the place, by reason that it was manured, we found to be more fruitful than the other part, especially the valleys among the hills.

Here we gave ourselves a little refreshing, as by very ripe and sweet grapes, which the fruitfulness of the earth at that season of the year yielded us: and that season being with us the depth of winter, it may seem strange that those fruits were then there growing: but the reason thereof is this, because they being between the Tropic and the Equinoctial, the sun passeth twice in the year through their zenith over their heads, by means whereof they have two summers, and being so near the heat of the line, they never lose the heat of the sun so much, but the fruits have their increase and continuance in the midst of winter. The island is wonderfully stored with goats and wild hens, and it hath salt also without labour, save only that the people gather it into heaps; which continually in great quantity is increased upon the sands by the flowing of the sea, and the receiving heat of the sun kerning the same, so that of the increase thereof they keep a continual traffic with their neighbours.

Amongst other things we found here a kind of fruit called cocos, which because it is not commonly known with us in England, I thought good to make some description of it.

The tree beareth no leaves nor branches, but at the

very top the fruit groweth in clusters, hard at the top
of the stem of the tree, as big every several fruit as a
man's head: but having taken off the uttermost bark,
which you shall find to be very full of strings or sinews,
as I may term them, you shall come to a hard shell
which may hold of quantity in liquor a pint commonly,
or some a quart, and some less. Within that shell of
the thickness of half an inch good, you shall have a
kind of hard substance and very white, no less good
and sweet than almonds: within that again a certain
clear liquor, which being drunk, you shall not only
find it very delicate and sweet, but most comfortable
and cordial.

After we had satisfied ourselves with some of these
fruits, we marched further into the island, and saw
great store of cabritos alive, which were so chased by
the inhabitants, that we could do no good towards our
provision, but they had laid out as it were to stop
our mouths withal, certain old dried cabritos, which
being but ill, and small and few, we made no account of.

Being returned to our ships, our General departed
hence the 31 of this month, and sailed by the island
of Santiago, but far enough from the danger of the inhabitants, who shot and discharged at us three pieces,
but they all fell short of us, and did us no harm. The
island is fair and large, and as it seemeth, rich and
fruitful, and inhabited by the Portugals, but the mountains and high places of the island are said to be
possessed by the Moors, who having been slaves to
the Portugals, to ease themselves, made escape to the
desert places of the island, where they abide with
great strength.

Being before this island, we espied two ships under

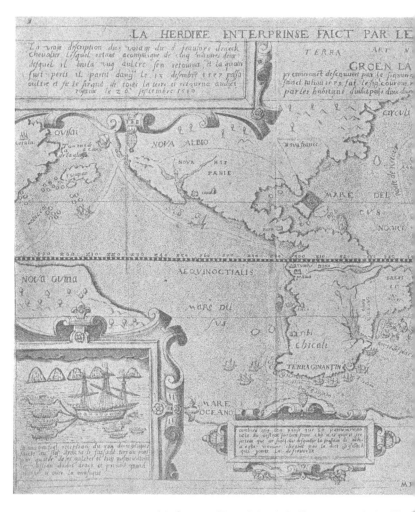

16th Century Map of Drake's Voyage round the Worl[...]
Moluccas, and of th[...]

*Note the statement that this map was seen and corrected [...]
and in Nova Albio, and marked the boundaries of t[...]*

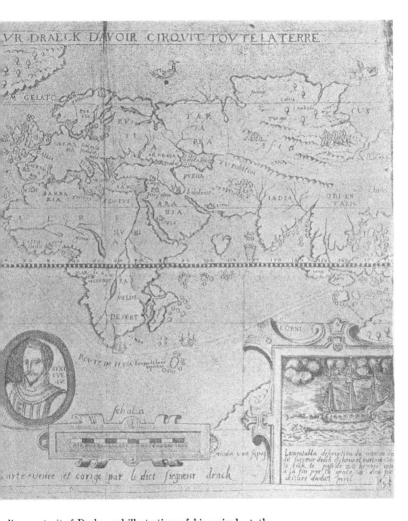

VR DRAECK DAVOIR CIRQVIT TOVTE LA TERRE

...ding portrait of Drake and illustrations of his **arrival at the**
n Hind on a rock).

e. He possibly added the coat-of-arms at **Elizabeth Island;**
r so as to give it a sea-board on the **Atlantic.**

sail, to the one of which we gave chase, and in the end boarded her with a ship-boat without resistance, which we found to be a good prize, and she yielded unto us good store of wine: which prize our General committed to the custody of Master Doughty, and retaining the pilot, sent the rest away with his pinnace, giving them a butt of wine and some victuals, and their wearing clothes, and so they departed.

The same night we came with the island called by the Portugals, Ilha del Fogo, that is, the burning island: in the north side whereof is a consuming fire. The matter is said to be of sulphur, but notwithstanding it is like to be a commodious island, because the Portugals have built, and do inhabit there.

Upon the south side thereof lieth a most pleasant and sweet island, the trees whereof are always green and fair to look upon, in respect whereof they call it Ilha Brava, that is, the brave island. From the banks thereof into the sea do run in many places reasonable streams of fresh waters easy to be come by, but there was no convenient road for our ships: for such was the depth, that no ground could be had for anchoring, and it is reported, that ground was never found in that place; so that the tops of Fogo burn not so high in the air, but the roots of Brava are quenched as low in the sea.

Being departed from these islands, we drew towards the line, where we were becalmed the space of 3 weeks, but yet subject to divers great storms, terrible lightnings and much thunder. But with this misery we had the commodity of great store of fish, as dolphins, bonitos, and flying fishes, whereof some fell into our ships, wherehence they could not rise again for want of moisture, for when their wings are dry, they cannot fly.

From the first day of our departure from the Islands of Cape Verde, we sailed 54 days without sight of land, and the first land that we fell with was the coast of Brazil, which we saw the fifth of April in the height of 33 degrees towards the pole Antarctic. And being discovered at sea by the inhabitants of the country, they made upon the coast great fires for a sacrifice (as we learned) to the devils; about which they use conjurations, making heaps of sand and other ceremonies, that when any ship shall go about to stay upon their coast, not only sands may be gathered together in shoals in every place, but also that storms and tempests may arise, to the casting away of ships and men, whereof (as it is reported) there have been divers experiments.

The seventh day in a mighty great storm both of lightning, rain, and thunder, we lost the canter which we called the *Christopher*: but the eleventh day after, by our General's great care in dispersing his ships, we found her again, and the place where we met, our General called the Cape of Joy, where every ship took in some water. Here we found a good temperature and sweet air, a very fair and pleasant country with an exceeding fruitful soil, where were great store of large and mighty deer, but we came not to the sight of any people: but travelling further into the country, we perceived the footing of people in the clay-ground, showing that they were men of great stature. Being returned to our ships, we weighed anchor, and ran somewhat further, and harboured ourselves between a rock and the main, where by means of the rock that brake the force of the sea, we rode very safe, and upon this rock we killed for our provision certain sea-wolves, commonly called with us seals.

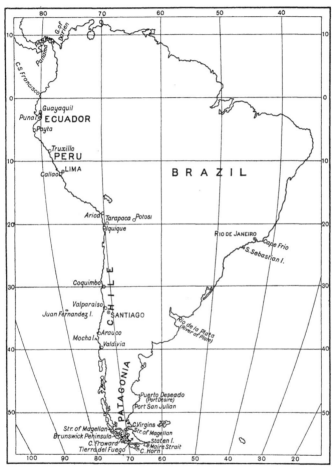

South America, to illustrate Magellan's, Drake's, and
Cavendish's Voyages.

From hence we went our course to 36 degrees, and entered the great river of Plate, and ran into 54 and 55 fathoms and a half of fresh water, where we filled our water by the ship's side : but our General finding here no good harbour, as he thought he should, bare out again to sea the 27 of April, and in bearing out we lost sight of our fly-boat wherein Master Doughty was. But we, sailing along, found a fair and reasonable good bay, wherein were many and the same profitable islands; one whereof had so many seals, as would at the least have laden all our ships, and the rest of the islands are, as it were, laden with fowls, which is wonderful to see, and they of divers sorts. It is a place very plentiful of victuals, and hath in it no want of fresh water.

Our General, after certain days of his abode in this place, being on shore in an island, the people of the country shewed themselves unto him, leaping and dancing, and entered into traffic with him, but they would not receive anything at any man's hands, but the same must be cast upon the ground. They are of clean, comely, and strong bodies, swift on foot, and seem to be very active.

The eighteenth day of May our General thought it needful to have a care of such ships as were absent, and therefore endeavouring to seek the fly-boat wherein Master Doughty was, we espied her again the next day. And whereas certain of our ships were sent to discover the coast and to search a harbour, the *Marigold* and the canter being employed in that business, came unto us and gave us understanding of a safe harbour that they had found. Wherewith all our ships bare, and entered it, where we watered and made new provision of victuals, as by seals, whereof we slew to the number of 200 or 300 in the space of an hour.

Here our General in the Admiral rode close aboard the fly-boat, and took out of her all the provision of victuals and what else was in her, and hauling her to the land, set fire to her, and so burnt her to save the iron work. Which being a-doing, there came down of the country certain of the people naked, saving only about their waist the skin of some beast with the fur or hair on, and something also wreathed on their heads: their faces were painted with divers colours, and some of them had on their heads the similitude of horns, every man his bow which was an ell in length, and a couple of arrows. They were very agile people and quick to deliver, and seemed not to be ignorant in the feats of wars, as by their order of ranging a few men, might appear. These people would not of a long time receive anything at our hands; yet at length our General being ashore, and they dancing after their accustomed manner about him, and he once turning his back towards them, one leaped suddenly to him, and took his cap with his gold band off his head, and ran a little distance from him and shared it with his fellow, the cap to the one, and the band to the other.

Having dispatched all our business in this place, we departed and set sail, and immediately upon our setting forth we lost our canter which was absent three or four days: but when our General had her again, he took out the necessaries, and so gave her over, near to the Cape of Good Hope.

The next day after, being the twentieth of June, we harboured ourselves again in a very good harbour, called by Magellan, Port St Julian, where we found a gibbet standing upon the main, which we supposed to be the place where Magellan did execution upon some of his disobedient and rebellious company.

The two and twentieth day our General went ashore to the main, and in his company John Thomas, and Robert Winterhie, Oliver the master-gunner, John Brewer, Thomas Hood, and Thomas Drake. And entering on land, they presently met with two or three of the country people, and Robert Winterhie having in his hands a bow and arrows, went about to make a shoot of pleasure, and in his draught his bow-string brake; which the rude savages taking as a token of war, began to bend the force of their bows against our company, and drove them to their shifts very narrowly.

In this port our General began to enquire diligently of the actions of Master Thomas Doughty, and found them not to be such as he looked for, but tending rather to contention or mutiny, or some other disorder, whereby (without redress) the success of the voyage might greatly have been hazarded: whereupon the company was called together and made acquainted with the particulars of the cause, which were found partly by Master Doughty's own confession, and partly by the evidence of the fact, to be true. Which when our General saw, although his private affection to Master Doughty (as he then in the presence of us all sacredly protested) was great, yet the care he had of the state of the voyage, of the expectation of her Majesty, and of the honour of his country did more touch him (as indeed it ought) than the private respect of one man. So that the cause being thoroughly heard, and all things done in good order as near as might be to the course of our laws in England, it was concluded that Master Doughty should receive punishment according to the quality of the offence. And he seeing no remedy but patience for himself, desired before his death to receive the communion, which he did at the hands of Master Fletcher, our minister, and our General himself accompanied him in that holy action. Which being done, and the place of execution made ready, he having embraced our General and taken his leave of all the company, with prayer for the Queen's Majesty and our realm, in quiet sort laid his head to the block, where he ended his life. This being done, our General made divers speeches to the whole company, persuading us to unity, obedience, love, and regard of our voyage; and for the better confirmation thereof, willed every man the next Sunday following to prepare himself to receive the communion, as Christian brethren and friends ought to do. Which was done in very reverent sort, and so with good contentment every man went about his business.

The 17 day of August we departed the port of St Julian, and the 20 day we fell with the Strait (or Freat) of Magellan, going into the South Sea; at the cape or headland whereof we found the body of a dead man, whose flesh was clean consumed.

The 21 day we entered the Strait, which we found to have many turnings, and as it were shuttings-up, as if there were no passage at all. By means whereof we had the wind often against us, so that some of the fleet recovering a cape or point of land, others should be forced to turn back again, and to come to an anchor where they could.

In this Strait there be many fair harbours, with

store of fresh water, but yet they lack their best commodity: for the water is there of such depth, that no man shall find ground to anchor in, except it be in some narrow river or corner, or between some rocks; so that if any extreme blasts or contrary winds do come (whereunto the place is much subject) it carrieth with it no small danger.

The land on both sides is very huge and mountainous; the lower mountains whereof, although they be monstrous and wonderful to look upon for their height, yet there are others which in height exceed them in a strange manner, reaching themselves above their fellows so high, that between them did appear three regions of clouds.

These mountains are covered with snow. At both the southerly and easterly parts of the Strait there are islands, among which the sea hath his indraught into the Straits, even as it hath in the main entrance of the Freat.

This Strait is extreme cold, with frost and snow continually; the trees seem to stoop with the burden of the weather, and yet are green continually, and many good and sweet herbs do very plentifully grow and increase under them.

The breadth of the Strait is in some places a league, in some other places 2 leagues, and three leagues, and in some other 4 leagues, but the narrowest place hath a league over.

The 24 of August we arrived at an island in the Straits, where we found great store of fowl which could not fly, of the bigness of geese, whereof we killed in less than one day 3000 and victualled ourselves thoroughly therewith.

The 6 day of September we entered the South Sea at the cape or head shore.

The seventh day we were driven by a great storm from the entering into the South Sea, two hundred leagues and odd in longitude, and one degree to the southward of the Strait: in which height, and so many leagues to the westward, the fifteenth day of September, fell out the eclipse of the moon at the hour of six of the clock at night. But neither did the ecliptical conflict of the moon impair our state, nor her clearing again amend us a whit, but the accustomed eclipse of the sea continued in his force, we being darkened more than the moon sevenfold.

From the bay (which we called The Bay of Severing of Friends) we were driven back to the southward of the straits in 57 degrees and a tierce: in which height we came to an anchor among the islands, having there fresh and very good water, with herbs of singular virtue. Not far from hence we entered another bay, where we found people both men and women in their canoes, naked, and ranging from one island to another to seek their meat; who entered traffic with us for such things as they had.

We returning hence northward again, found the 3 of October three islands, in one of which was such plenty of birds as is scant credible to report.

The 8 day of October we lost sight of one of our consorts wherein Master Winter was, who as then we supposed was put by a storm into the Straits again. Which at our return home we found to be true, and he not perished, as some of our company feared.

Thus being come into the height of the Straits again, we ran, supposing the coast of Chili to lie as the general

Fletcher's Map of Three Islands discovered by Drake
Note that the South is at the top of the map

maps have described it, namely north-west; which we found to lie and trend to the north-east and eastwards. Whereby it appeareth that this part of Chili hath not been truly hitherto discovered, or at the least not truly reported for the space of 12 degrees at the least, being set down either of purpose to deceive, or of ignorant conjecture.

We continuing our course, fell the 29 of November with an island called La Mocha, where we cast anchor, and our General hoising out our boat, went with ten of our company to shore, where we found people, whom the cruel and extreme dealings of the Spaniards have forced for their own safety and liberty to flee from the main, and to fortify themselves in this island. We being on land, the people came down to us to the water side with show of great courtesy, bringing to us potatoes, roots, and two very fat sheep, which our General received and gave them other things for them, and had promise to have water there. But the next day repairing again to the shore, and sending two men a-land with barrels to fill water, the people taking them for Spaniards (to whom they use to show no favour if they take them) laid violent hands on them, and as we think, slew them.

Our General seeing this, stayed here no longer, but weighed anchor, and set sail towards the coast of Chili. And drawing towards it, we met near to the shore an Indian in a canoa, who thinking us to have been Spaniards, came to us and told us, that at a place called Santiago, there was a great Spanish ship laden from the kingdom of Peru: for which good news our General gave him divers trifles, whereof he was glad, and went along with us and brought us to the place, which is called the port of Valparaiso.

When we came thither, we found indeed the ship riding at anchor, having in her eight Spaniards and three negroes, who thinking us to have been Spaniards and their friends, welcomed us with a drum, and made ready a botija of wine of Chili to drink to us. But as soon as we were entered, one of our company called Thomas Moon began to lay about him, and struck one of the Spaniards, and said unto him, " Abaxo Perro," that is in English, " Go down, dog."   One of these Spaniards seeing persons of that quality in those seas, all to crossed, and blessed himself : but to be short, we stowed them under hatches, all save one Spaniard, who suddenly and desperately leaped overboard into the sea, and swam ashore to the town of Santiago, to give them warning of our arrival.

They of the town, being not above 9 households, presently fled away and abandoned the town. Our General manned his boat, and the Spanish ship's boat, and went to the town, and being come to it, we rifled it, and came to a small chapel which we entered, and found therein a silver chalice, two cruets, and one altar-cloth, the spoil whereof our General gave to Master Fletcher, his minister.

We found also in this town a warehouse stored with wine of Chili, and many boards of cedar-wood ; all which wine we brought away with us, and certain of the boards to burn for fire-wood. And so being come aboard, we departed the haven, having first set all the Spaniards on land, saving one John Griego, a Greek born, whom our General carried with him for his pilot to bring him into the haven of Lima.

When we were at sea, our General rifled the ship, and found in her good store of the wine of Chili, and 25,000 pesos of very pure and fine gold of Valdivia, amounting in value to 37,000 ducats of Spanish money, and above. So going on our course, we arrived next at a place called Coquimbo, where our General sent 14 of his men on land to fetch water: but they were espied by the Spaniards, who came with 300 horsemen and 200 footmen, and slew one of our men with a piece. The rest came aboard in safety, and the Spaniards departed. We went on shore again, and buried our man, and the Spaniards came down again with a flag of truce, but we set sail and would not trust them.

From hence we went to a certain port called Tarapaca, where being landed, we found by the sea side a Spaniard lying asleep, who had lying by him 13 bars of silver, which weighed 4000 ducats Spanish. We took the silver, and left the man.

Not far from hence going on land for fresh water, we met with a Spaniard and an Indian boy driving 8 llamas or sheep of Peru, which are as big as asses; every of which sheep had on his back 2 bags of leather, each bag containing 50 lb. weight of fine silver: so that bringing both the sheep and their burden to the ships, we found in all the bags 800 weight of silver.

Here hence we sailed to a place called Arica, and being entered the port, we found there three small barks which we rifled, and found in one of them 57 wedges of silver, each of them weighing about 20 pound weight, and every of these wedges were of the fashion and bigness of a brickbat. In all these 3 barks we found not one person: for they mistrusting no strangers, were all gone a-land to the town, which consisteth of about twenty houses, which we would have ransacked if our company had been better and more in number.   But our General, contented with the spoil of the ships, left the town and put off again to sea, and set sail for Lima, and by the way met with a small bark, which he boarded, and found in her good store of linen cloth.   Whereof taking some quantity, he let her go.

To Lima we came the 13 day of February, and being entered the haven, we found there about twelve sail of ships lying fast moored at an anchor, having all their sails carried on shore; for the masters and merchants were here most secure, having never been assaulted by enemies, and at this time feared the approach of none such as we were.   Our General rifled these ships, and found in one of them a chest full of reals of plate, and good store of silks and linen cloth, and took the chest into his own ship, and good store of the silks and linen. In which ship he had news of another ship called the *Cacafuego*, which was gone towards Payta, and that the same ship was laden with treasure.   Whereupon we stayed no longer here, but cutting all the cables of the ships in the haven, we let them drive whither they would, either to sea or to the shore, and with all speed we followed the *Cacafuego* toward Payta, thinking there to have found her: but before we arrived there, she was gone from thence towards Panama; whom our General still pursued, and by the way met with a bark laden with ropes and tackle for ships, which he boarded and searched, and found in her 80 lb. weight of gold, and a crucifix of gold with goodly great emeralds set in it, which he took, and some of the cordage also for his own ship.

From hence we departed, still following the *Cacafuego*, and our General promised our company, that whosoever could first descry her, should have his chain of gold for his good news. It fortuned that John Drake going up into the top, descried her about three of the clock, and about six of the clock we came to her and boarded her, and shot at her three pieces of ordnance, and strake down her mizen; and being entered, we found in her great riches, as jewels and precious stones, thirteen chests full of reals of plate, fourscore pound weight of gold, and six-and-twenty ton of silver. The place where we took this prize, was called Cape de San Francisco, about 150 leagues from Panama.

The pilot's name of this ship was Francisco, and amongst other plate that our General found in this ship, he found two very fair gilt bowls of silver, which were the pilot's. To whom our General said: "Señor Pilot, you have here two silver cups, but I must needs have one of them": which the pilot, because he could not otherwise choose, yielded unto, and gave the other to the steward of our General's ships.

When this pilot departed from us, his boy said thus unto our General: "Captain, our ship shall be called no more the *Cacafuego*, but the *Cacaplata*, and your ship shall be called the *Cacafuego*." Which pretty speech of the pilot's boy ministered matter of laughter to us, both then and long after.

When our General had done what he would with this *Cacafuego*, he cast her off, and we went on our course still towards the west, and not long after met with a ship laden with linen cloth and fine China dishes of white earth, and great store of China silks, of all which things we took as we listed.

The owner himself of this ship was in her, who was

a Spanish gentleman, from whom our General took a
falcon of gold, with a great emerald in the breast
thereof; and the pilot of the ship he took also with
him, and so cast the ship off.

This pilot brought us to the haven of Guatulco, the
town whereof, as he told us, had but 17 Spaniards in
it.   As soon as we were entered this haven, we landed,

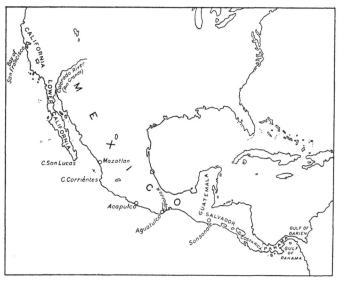

Part of North and Central America to illustrate
Drake's and Cavendish's voyages

and went presently to the town, and to the Town-house,
where we found a judge sitting in judgment, being
associate with three other officers, upon three negroes
that had conspired the burning of the town: both
which judges and prisoners we took, and brought them
a-shipboard, and caused the chief judge to write his
letter to the town, to command all the townsmen to

avoid, that we might safely water there. Which being done, and they departed, we ransacked the town, and in one house we found a pot of the quantity of a bushel, full of reals of plate, which we brought to our ship.

And here one Thomas Moon, one of our company, took a Spanish gentleman as he was flying out of the town, and searching him, he found a chain of gold about him, and other jewels, which he took, and so let him go.

At this place our General, among other Spaniards, set ashore his Portugal pilot, which he took at the Islands of Cape Verde, out of a ship of St Mary port, of Portugal. And having set them ashore, we departed hence, and sailed to the Island of Canno, where our General landed, and brought to shore his own ship, and discharged her, mended, and graved her, and furnished our ship with water and wood sufficiently.

And while we were here, we espied a ship, and set sail after her, and took her, and found in her two pilots, and a Spanish Governor, going for the Islands of the Philippinas: we searched the ship, and took some of her merchandise, and so let her go. Our General at this place and time, thinking himself both in respect of his private injuries received from the Spaniards, as also of their contempts and indignities offered to our country and Prince in general, sufficiently satisfied, and re-venged: and supposing that her Majesty at his return would rest contented with this service, purposed to continue no longer upon the Spanish coasts, but began to consider and to consult of the best way for his country.

He thought it not good to return by the Straits, for two special causes: the one, lest the Spaniards should there wait, and attend for him in great number and strength, whose hands, he, being left but one ship, could not possibly escape. The other cause was the dangerous situation of the mouth of the Straits in the South Sea, where continual storms reigning and blustering, as he found by experience, besides the shoals and sands upon the coast, he thought it not a good course to adventure that way. He resolved therefore to avoid these hazards, to go forward to the Islands of the Malucos, and there-hence to sail the course of the Portugals by the Cape of Buena Esperanza.

Upon this resolution, he began to think of his best way to the Malucos, and finding himself, where he now was, becalmed, he saw that of necessity he must be forced to take a Spanish course, namely to sail some-what northerly to get a wind. We therefore set sail, and sailed 600 leagues at the least for a good wind, and thus much we sailed from the 16 of April, till the 3 of June.

The 5 day of June, being in 43 degrees towards the pole Arctic, we found the air so cold, that our men being grievously pinched with the same, complained of the extremity thereof, and the further we went, the more the cold increased upon us. Whereupon we thought it best for that time to seek the land, and did so, finding it not mountainous, but low plain land, till we came within 38 degrees towards the line. In which height it pleased God to send us into a fair and good bay, with a good wind to enter the same.

In this bay we anchored, and the people of the country having their houses close by the water's side, shewed themselves unto us, and sent a present to our General.

When they came unto us, they greatly wondered at the things that we brought, but our General (according to his natural and accustomed humanity) courteously entreated them, and liberally bestowed on them necessary things to cover their nakedness; whereupon they supposed us to be gods, and would not be persuaded to the contrary. The presents which they sent to our General, were feathers, and cauls of net-work.

Their houses are digged round about with earth, and have from the uttermost brims of the circle, clefts of wood set upon them, joining close together at the top like a spire steeple, which by reason of that closeness are very warm.

Their bed is the ground with rushes strewed on it, and lying about the house, have the fire in the midst. The men go naked; the women take bulrushes, and kemb them after the manner of hemp, and thereof make their loose garments, which being knit about their middles, hang down about their hips, having also about their shoulders a skin of deer, with the hair upon it. These women are very obedient and serviceable to their husbands.

After they were departed from us, they came and visited us the second time, and brought with them feathers and bags of tobacco for presents. And when they came to the top of the hill (at the bottom whereof we had pitched our tents), they stayed themselves: where one appointed for speaker wearied himself with making a long oration; which done, they left their bows upon the hill, and came down with their presents.

In the meantime the women, remaining on the hill, tormented themselves lamentably, tearing their flesh from their cheeks, whereby we perceived that they were about a sacrifice. In the meantime our General with his company went to prayer, and to reading of the Scriptures, at which exercise they were attentive, and seemed greatly to be affected with it: but when they were come unto us, they restored again unto us those things which before we bestowed upon them.

The news of our being there being spread through the country, the people that inhabited round about came down, and amongst them the king himself, a man of a goodly stature, and comely personage, with many other tall and warlike men: before whose coming were sent two ambassadors to our General, to signify that their king was coming. In doing of which message, their speech was continued about half an hour. This ended, they by signs requested our General to send something by their hand to their king, as a token that his coming might be in peace: wherein our General having satisfied them, they returned with glad tidings to their king, who marched to us with a princely majesty, the people crying continually after their manner, and as they drew near unto us, so did they strive to behave themselves in their actions with comeliness.

In the fore-front was a man of a goodly personage, who bare the sceptre or mace before the king, whereupon hanged two crowns, a less and a bigger, with three chains of a marvellous length. The crowns were made of knit work wrought artificially with feathers of divers colours: the chains were made of a bony substance, and few be the persons among them that are admitted to wear them; and of that number also the persons are stinted, as some ten, some 12, etc. Next unto him which bare the sceptre, was the king himself, with his guard about his person, clad with coney skins, and other skins. After them followed the naked common sort of people, every one having his face painted, some with white, some with black, and other colours, and having in their hands one thing or another for a present. Not so much as their children, but they also brought their presents.

In the meantime our General gathered his men together, and marched within his fenced place, making against their approaching a very warlike show. They being trooped together in their order, and a general salutation being made, there was presently a general silence. Then he that bare the sceptre before the king, being informed by another, whom they assigned to that office, with a manly and lofty voice proclaimed that which the other spake to him in secret, continuing half an hour: which ended, and a general Amen, as it were, given, the king with the whole number of men and women (the children excepted) came down without any weapon; who, descending to the foot of the hill, set themselves in order.

In coming towards our bulwarks and tents, the sceptre-bearer began a song, observing his measures in a dance, and that with a stately countenance; whom the king with his guard, and every degree of persons, following, did in like manner sing and dance, saving only the women, which danced and kept silence. The General permitted them to enter within our bulwark, where they continued their song and dance a reasonable time. When they had satisfied themselves, they made signs to our General to sit down; to whom the king, and divers others made several orations, or rather supplications, that he would take their province and

kingdom into his hand, and become their king, making
signs that they would resign unto him their right and
title of the whole land, and become his subjects.   In
which, to persuade us the better, the king and the rest,
with one consent, and with great reverence, joyfully
singing a song, did set the crown upon his· head, en-
riched his neck with all their chains, and offered unto
him many other things, honouring him by the name
of Hioh, adding thereunto as it seemed, a sign of
triumph: which thing our General thought not meet
to reject, because he knew not what honour and profit
it might be to our country.   Wherefore in the name,
and to the use of her Majesty, he took the sceptre,
crown, and dignity of the said country into his hands,
wishing that the riches and treasure thereof might so
conveniently be transported to the enriching of her
kingdom at home, as it aboundeth in the same.

The common sort of people leaving the king and his
guard with our General, scattered themselves together
with their sacrifices among our people, taking a diligent
view of every person: and such as pleased their fancy
(which were the youngest), they enclosing them about
offered their sacrifices unto them with lamentable
weeping, scratching and tearing the flesh from their
faces with their nails, whereof issued abundance of
blood.   But we used signs to them of disliking this,
and stayed their hands from force, and directed them
upwards to the living God, whom only they ought to
worship.   They shewed unto us their wounds, and
craved help of them at our hands; whereupon we gave
them lotions, plasters, and ointments, agreeing to the
state of their griefs, beseeching God to cure their
diseases.   Every third day they brought their sacrifices

unto us, until they understood our meaning, that we had no pleasure in them: yet they could not be long absent from us, but daily frequented our company to the hour of our departure, which departure seemed so grievous unto them, that their joy was turned into sorrow. They entreated us, that being absent we would remember them, and by stealth provided a sacrifice, which we misliked.

Our necessary business being ended, our General with his company travelled up into the country to their villages, where we found herds of deer by a thousand in a company, being most large, and fat of body.

We found the whole country to be a warren of a strange kind of coneys, their bodies in bigness as be the Barbary coneys, their heads as the heads of ours, the feet of a want, and the tail of a rat, being of great length. Under her chin is on either side a bag, into the which she gathereth her meat, when she hath filled her belly abroad. The people eat their bodies, and make great account of their skins, for their king's coat was made of them.

Our General called this country Nova Albion, and that for two causes: the one in respect of the white banks and cliffs, which lie towards the sea: and the other, because it might have some affinity with our country in name, which sometime was so called.

There is no part of earth here to be taken up, wherein there is not some probable show of gold or silver.

At our departure hence our General set up a monument of our being there, as also of her Majesty's right and title to the same, namely a plate, nailed upon a fair great post, whereupon was engraven her Majesty's name, the day and year of our arrival there, with the free giving up of the province and people into her Majesty's hands, together with her Highness's picture and arms, in a piece of sixpence of current English money, under the plate, whereunder was also written the name of our General.

It seemeth that the Spaniards hitherto had never been in this part of the country, neither did ever discover the land by many degrees, to the southwards of this place.

After we had set sail from hence, we continued without sight of land till the 13 day of October following, which day in the morning we fell with certain islands 8 degrees to the northward of the line, from which islands came a great number of canoas, having in some of them 4, in some 6, and in some also 14 men, bringing with them cocos, and other fruits. Their canoas were hollow within, and cut with great art and cunning, being very smooth within and without, and bearing a glass as if it were a horn daintily burnished, having a prow and a stern of one sort, yielding inward circle-wise, being of a great height, and full of certain white shells for a bravery, and on each side of them lie out two pieces of timber about a yard and a half long, more or less, according to the smallness, or bigness of the boat.

This people have the nether part of their ears cut into a round circle, hanging down very low upon their cheeks, whereon they hang things of a reasonable weight. The nails of their hands are an inch long, their teeth are as black as pitch, and they renew them often, by eating of a herb with a kind of powder, which they always carry about them in a cane for the same purpose.

Leaving this island the night after we fell with it, the 18 of October we lighted upon divers others, some whereof made a great show of inhabitants.

We continued our course by the Islands of Tagulada, Zelon, and Zewarra, being friends to the Portugals, the first whereof hath growing in it great store of cinnamon.

The 14 of November we fell with the Islands of Maluco. Which day at night (having directed our course to run with Tidore) in coasting along the Island of Mutyr, belonging to the king of Ternate, his deputy or vice-king seeing us at sea, came with his canoa to us without all fear, and came aboard, and after some conference with our General, willed him in any wise to run in with Ternate, and not with Tidore, assuring him that the king would be glad of his coming, and would be ready to do what he would require, for which purpose he himself would that night be with the king, and tell him the news. With whom if he once dealt, he should find that as he was a king, so his word should stand: adding further, that if he went to Tidore before he came to Ternate, the king would have nothing to do with us, because he held the Portugal as his enemy. Whereupon our General resolved to run with Ternate, where the next morning early we came to anchor, at which time our General sent a messenger to the king with a velvet cloak for a present, and token of his coming to be in peace, and that he required nothing but traffic and exchange of merchandise, whereof he had good store, in such things as he wanted.

In the meantime the vice-king had been with the king according to his promise, signifying unto him what good things he might receive from us by traffic: whereby the king was moved with great liking towards us, and sent to our General with special message, that he should have what things he needed and would require, with peace and friendship; and moreover that he would yield himself, and the right of his island to be at the pleasure and commandment of so famous a prince as we served. In token whereof he sent to our General a signet, and within short time after came in his own person, with boats and canoas, to our ship, to bring her into a better and safer road than she was in at present.

In the meantime, our General's messenger being come to the Court, was met by certain noble personages with great solemnity, and brought to the king, at whose hands he was most friendly and graciously entertained.

The king purposing to come to our ship, sent before 4 great and large canoas, in every one whereof were certain of his greatest states that were about him, attired in white lawn of cloth of Calicut, having over their heads from the one end of the canoa to the other, a covering of thin perfumed mats, borne up with a frame made of reeds for the same use; under which every one did sit in his order according to his dignity, to keep him from the heat of the sun; divers of whom being of good age and gravity, did make an ancient and fatherly show. There were also divers young and comely men attired in white, as were the others: the rest were soldiers, which stood in comely order round about on both sides. Without whom sat the rowers in certain galleries, which being three on a side all along the canoas, did lie off from the side thereof three or four yards, one being orderly builded lower than another, in every of which galleries were the number of 4 score rowers.

These canoas were furnished with warlike munition, every man for the most part having his sword and target, with his dagger, beside other weapons, as lances, calivers, darts, bows and arrows: also every canoa had a small cast base mounted at the least one full yard upon a stock set upright.

Thus coming near our ship, in order they rowed about us, one after another, and passing by, did their homage with great solemnity, the great personages beginning with great gravity and fatherly countenances, signifying that the king had sent them to conduct our ship into a better road.

Soon after the king himself repaired, accompanied with 6 grave and ancient persons, who did their obeisance with marvellous humility. The king was a man of tall stature, and seemed to be much delighted with the sound of our music; to whom as also to his nobility, our General gave presents, wherewith they were passing well contented.

At length the king craved leave of our General to depart, promising the next day to come aboard, and in the meantime to send us such victuals, as were necessary for our provision: so that the same night we received of them meal, which they call sago, made of the tops of certain trees, tasting in the mouth like sour curds, but melteth like sugar, whereof they make certain cakes, which may be kept the space of ten years, and yet then good to be eaten. We had of them store of rice, hens, unperfect and liquid sugar, sugar-canes, and a fruit which they call figo, with store of cloves.

The king having promised to come aboard, brake his promise, but sent his brother to make his excuse, and to entreat our General to come on shore, offering himself pawn aboard for his safe return. Whereunto our General consented not, upon mislike conceived of the breach of his promise, the whole company also utterly refusing it. But to satisfy him, our General sent certain of his gentlemen to the Court, to accompany the king's brother, reserving the vice-king for their safe return. They were received of another brother of the king's, and other states, and were conducted with great honour to the castle. The place that they were brought unto, was a large and fair house, where were at the least 1000 persons assembled.

The king being yet absent, there sat in their places 60 grave personages, all which were said to be of the king's council. There were besides 4 grave persons, apparelled all in red, down to the ground, and attired on their heads like the Turks, and these were said to be Romans, and ligiers there to keep continual traffic with the people of Ternate. There were also 2 Turks ligiers in this place, and one Italian. The king at last came in guarded with 12 lances, covered over with a rich canopy with embossed gold. Our men accompanied with one of their captains called Moro, rising to meet him, he graciously did welcome, and entertain them. He was attired after the manner of the country, but more sumptuously than the rest. From his waist down to the ground, was all cloth of gold, and the same very rich: his legs were bare, but on his feet were a pair of shoes, made of Cordovan skin. In the attire of his head were finely wreathed hooped rings of gold, and about his neck he had a chain of perfect gold, the links whereof were great, and one fold double. On his fingers he had six very fair jewels, and sitting in his chair of state, at his right hand stood a page with a fan in his hand, breathing and gathering the air to the king. The fan was in length two foot, and in breadth one foot, set with 8 sapphires, richly embroidered, and knit to a staff 3 foot in length, by the which the page did hold, and move it. Our gentlemen having delivered their message, and received order accordingly, were licensed to depart, being safely conducted back again by one of the king's council.

This island is the chiefest of all the Islands of Maluco, and the king hereof is king of 70 islands besides. The king with his people are Moors in religion, observing certain new moons, with fastings: during which fasts, they neither eat nor drink in the day, but in the night.

After that our gentlemen were returned, and that we had here by the favour of the king received all necessary things that the place could yield us: our General considering the great distance, and how far he was yet off from his country, thought it not best here to linger the time any longer, but weighing his anchors, set out of the island, and sailed to a certain little island to the southwards of Celebes, where we graved our ship, and continued there in that and other businesses 26 days. This island is thoroughly grown with wood of a large and high growth, very straight and without boughs, save only in the head or top, whose leaves are not much differing from our broom in England. Amongst these trees night by night, through the whole land, did show themselves an infinite swarm of fiery worms flying in the air, whose bodies being no bigger than our common English flies, make such a show and light, as if every twig or tree had been a burning candle. In this place breedeth also wonderful store of bats, as big as large hens: of crayfishes also here wanted no plenty, and they of exceeding bigness, one whereof was sufficient for 4 hungry stomachs at a dinner, being also very good and restoring meat, whereof we had experience: and they dig themselves holes in the earth like coneys.

When we had ended our business here, we weighed, and set sail to run for the Malucos. But having at that time a bad wind, and being amongst the islands, with much difficulty we recovered to the northward of the Island of Celebes, where by reason of contrary winds, not able to continue our course to run westwards, we were enforced to alter the same to the southward again, finding that course also to be very hard and dangerous for us, by reason of infinite shoals which lie off, and among the islands: whereof we had too much trial, to the hazard and danger of our ship and lives. For, of all other days, upon the 9 of January, in the year 1579, we ran suddenly upon a rock, where we stuck fast from 8 of the clock at night till 4 of the clock in the afternoon the next day, being indeed out of all hope to escape the danger. But our General as he had always hitherto showed himself courageous, and of a good confidence in the mercy and protection of God, so now he continued in the same, and lest he should seem to perish wilfully, both he and we did our best endeavour to save ourselves; which it pleased God so to bless, that in the end we cleared ourselves most happily of the danger.

We lighted our ship upon the rocks of 3 ton of

cloves, 8 pieces of ordnance, and certain meal and beans: and then the wind (as it were in a moment by the special grace of God) changing from the starboard to the larboard of the ship, we hoised our sails, and the happy gale drove our ship off the rock into the sea again, to the no little comfort of all our hearts, for which we gave God such praise and thanks, as so great a benefit required.

The 8 of February following, we fell with the fruitful Island of Barateve, having in the meantime suffered many dangers by winds and shoals. The people of this island are comely in body and stature, and of a civil behaviour, just in dealing, and courteous to strangers; whereof we had the experience sundry ways, they being most glad of our presence, and very ready to relieve our wants in those things which their country did yield. The men go naked, saving their heads and middles, every man having something or other hanging at their ears. Their women are covered from the middle down to the foot, wearing a great number of bracelets upon their arms, for some had 8 upon each arm, being made some of bone, some of horn, and some of brass, the lightest whereof by our estimation weighed two ounces apiece.

With this people linen-cloth is good merchandise, and of good request, whereof they make rolls for their heads, and girdles to wear about them.

Their island is both rich and fruitful: rich in gold, silver, copper, and sulphur, wherein they seem skilful and expert, not only to try the same, but in working it also artificially into any form and fashion that pleaseth them.

Their fruits be divers and plentiful; as nutmegs,

ginger, long pepper, lemons, cucumbers, cocos, figos, sago, with divers other sorts. And, among all the rest, we had one fruit, in bigness, form, and husk, like a bay berry, hard of substance, and pleasant of taste, which being sodden, becometh soft, and is a most good and wholesome victual, whereof we took reasonable store, as we did also of the other fruits and spices: so that to confess a truth, since the time that we first set out of our own country of England, we happened upon no place (Ternate only excepted) wherein we found more comforts and better means of refreshing.

At our departure from Barateve, we set our course for Java Major, where arriving, we found great courtesy, and honourable entertainment. This island is governed by 5 kings, whom they call Rajah: as Rajah Donaw, and Rajah Mang Bange, and Rajah Cabuccapollo, which live as having one spirit, and one mind.

Of these five we had four a-shipboard at once, and two or three often. They are wonderfully delighted in coloured clothes, as red and green: the upper parts of their bodies are naked, save their heads, whereupon they wear a Turkish roll, as do the Maluccians. From the middle downward they wear a pintado of silk, trailing upon the ground, in colour as they best like.

The Maluccians hate that their women should be seen of strangers: but these offer them of high courtesy, yea, the kings themselves.

The people are of goodly stature, and warlike, well provided of swords and targets, with daggers, all being of their own work, and most artificially done, both in tempering their metal, as also in the form; whereof we bought reasonable store.

They have a house in every village for their common

assembly : every day they meet twice, men, women, and children, bringing with them such victuals as they think good, some fruits, some rice boiled, some hens roasted, some sago, having a table made 3 foot from the ground, whereon they set their meat, that every person sitting at the table may eat, one rejoicing in the company of another.

They boil their rice in an earthen pot, made in form of a sugar loaf, being full of holes, as our pots which we water our gardens withal, and it is open at the great end, wherein they put their rice dry, without any moisture. In the meantime they have ready another great earthen pot, set fast in a furnace, boiling full of water, whereinto they put their pot with rice, by such measure, that they swelling become soft at the first, and by their swelling stopping the holes of the pot, admit no more water to enter, but the more they are boiled, the harder and more firm substance they become. So that in the end they are a firm and good bread, of the which with oil, butter, sugar, and other spices, they make divers sorts of meats very pleasant of taste, and nourishing to nature.

Not long before our departure, they told us that not far off there were such great ships as ours, wishing us to beware : upon this our captain would stay no longer.

From Java Major we sailed for the Cape of Good Hope, which was the first land we fell withal : neither did we touch with it, or any other land, until we came to Sierra Leona, upon the coast of Guinea ; notwithstanding we ran hard aboard the Cape, finding the report of the Portugals to be most false, who affirm that it is the most dangerous cape of the world, never without intolerable storms and present danger to travellers, which come near the same.

This cape is a most stately thing, and the fairest cape we saw in the whole circumference of the earth, and we passed by it the 18 of June.

From thence we continued our course to Sierra Leona, on the coast of Guinea, where we arrived the 22 of July, and found necessary provisions, great store of elephants, oysters upon trees of one kind, spawning and increasing infinitely, the oyster suffering no bud to grow. We departed thence the 24 day.

We arrived in England the third of November 1580, being the third year of our departure.

Sir Thomas Cavendish

CAVENDISH. FIRST VOYAGE

The admirable and prosperous voyage of the Worshipful
Master Thomas Cavendish, of Trimley, in the
County of Suffolk, Esquire, into the South Sea,
and from thence round about the circumference of
the whole earth; begun in the year of our Lord
1586, and finished 1588. Written by Master
Francis Pretty, lately of Eye, in Suffolk, a gentleman employed in the same action.

We departed out of Plymouth on Thursday, the 21 of
July, 1586, with 3 sails, to wit, the *Desire*, a ship of
120 tons, the *Content*, of 60 tons, and the *Hugh Gallant*,
a bark of 40 tons: in which small fleet were 123
persons of all sorts, with all kind of furniture and
victuals sufficient for the space of two years, at the
charges of the worshipful Master Thomas Cavendish of
Trimley, in the County of Suffolk, Esquire, being our
General.

On Tuesday, the 26 of the same month, we were 45
leagues from Cape Finis-terrae, where we met with 5 sails
of Biscayans, coming from the Grand Bay in Newfoundland, as we supposed, which our Admiral shot at, and
fought with them 3 hours, but we took none of them
by reason the night grew on.

The first of August we came in sight of Forteventura,
one of the isles of the Canaries, about ten of the clock
in the morning.

On Sunday, being the 7 of August, we were gotten as high as Rio del Oro, on the coast of Barbary.

On Monday, the 19, we fell with Cape Blanco: but the wind blew so much at the North, that we could not get up where the canters do use to ride and fish: therefore we lay off 6 hours west-south-west, because of the sand which lieth off the cape south-west and by south.

The 15 day of the same month we were in the height of Cape Verde, by estimation 50 leagues off the same.

The 18 Sierra Leona did bear east of us, being 45 leagues from us: and the same day the wind shifted to the north-west, so that by the 20 day of the said month we were in 6½ degrees to the northward, from the equinoctial line.

The 23 we put room for Sierra Leona, and the 25 day we fell with the point on the south side of Sierra Leona, which Master Brewer knew very well, and went in before with the *Content*, which was Vice-admiral: and we had no less than 5 fathoms water when we had least, and had for 14 leagues in south-west all the way running into the harbour of Sierra Leona, 16, 14, 12, 10, and 8 fathoms of water.

The 26 of the said month we put into the harbour, and in going in we had (by the southernmost point when we had least) 5 fathoms water fair by the rock as it lieth at the said point, and after we came 2 or 3 cables' length within the said rock, we never had less than 10 fathoms, until we came up to the road, which is about a league from the point, borrowing always on the south side until you come up to the watering-place, in which bay is the best road; but you must ride far into the bay, because there run marvellous great tides in the offing, and it floweth into the road next of anything at a south-east and by east moon.

It is out of England to this place 930 leagues: which we ran from the 21 of July to the 26 of this month of August.

On Saturday, being the 27 day, there came 2 negroes aboard our Admiral from the shore, and made signs unto our General that there was a Portugal ship up within the harbour; so the *Hugh Gallant*, being the Rear-admiral, went up 3 or 4 leagues, but for want of a pilot they sought no farther: for the harbour runneth 3 or 4 leagues up more, and is of a marvellous breadth and very dangerous, as we learned afterward by a Portugal.

On Sunday, the 28, the General sent some of his company on shore, and there as they played and danced all the forenoon among the negroes, to the end to have heard some good news of the Portugal ship, toward their coming aboard they espied a Portugal, which lay hid among the bushes, whom we took and brought away with us the same night: and he told us it was very dangerous going up with our boats for to seek the ship that was at the town. Whereupon we went not to seek her, because we knew he told us the truth: for we bound him and made him fast, and so examined him. Also he told us that his ship was there cast away, and that there were two more of his company among the negroes. The Portugal's name was Emmanuel, and was by his occupation a caulker, belonging to the Port of Portugal.

On Monday morning, being the 29 day, our General landed with 70 men or thereabout, and went up to their town, where we burnt 2 or 3 houses, and took what spoil we would, which was but little; but all the people fled, and in our retiring aboard in a very little plain at their town's end they shot their arrows at us out of the woods, and hurt 3 or 4 of our men. Their arrows were poisoned, but yet none of our men miscarried at that time, thanked be God. Their town is marvellous artificially builded with mud walls, and built round, with their yards paled in and kept very clean as well in their streets as in their houses. These negroes use good obedience to their king, as one of our men said, which was with them in pawn for the negroes which came first. There were in their town by estimation about one hundred houses.

The first of September there went many of our men on shore at the watering-place, and did wash shirts very quietly all the day: and the second day they went again, and the negroes were in ambush round about the place: and the carpenter of the Admiral going into the wood to do some special business, espied them by good fortune. But the negroes rushed out upon our men so suddenly, that in retiring to our boats many of them were hurt; among whom one William Pickman, a soldier, was shot into the thigh, who, plucking the arrow out, broke it, and left the head behind; and he told the chirurgeons that he plucked out all the arrow, because he would not have them lance his thigh: whereupon the poison wrought so that night, that he was marvellously swollen, and the next morning he died, the piece of the arrow with the poison being plucked out of his thigh.

The third day of the said month, divers of our fleet went up 4 miles within the harbour with our boat, and caught great store of fish, and went on shore and took lemons from the trees, and coming aboard again, saw two buffes.

The 6 day we departed from Sierra Leona, and went out of the harbour, and stayed one tide 3 leagues from the point of the mouth of the harbour in 6 fathoms, and it floweth south-south-west.

On Wednesday, being the 7 of the same month, we departed from one of the Isles of Cape Verde, *alias* the Isles of Madrabumba, which is 10 leagues distant from the point of Sierra Leona : and about five of the clock the same night we anchored 2 miles off the island in 6 fathoms water, and landed the same night, and found plantains only upon the island.

The 8 day one of our boats went out and sounded round about the island, and they passed through a sound at the west end of the island, where they found 5 fathoms round about the island, until they came unto the very gut of the sound, and then for a cast or two they had but two fathoms, and presently after, 6 fathoms, and so deeper and deeper. And at the east end of the island there was a town, where negroes do use at sometimes, as we perceived by their provision.

There is no fresh water on all the south side, as we could perceive, but on the north side three or four very good places of fresh water : and all the whole island is a wood, save certain little places where their houses stand, which are environed round about with plantain-trees, whereof the fruit is excellent meat. This place is subject marvellous much to thunder, rain, and lightning in this month. I think the reason is, because the sun is so near the line equinoctial.

On Saturday, the tenth, we departed from the said

island about 3 of the clock in the afternoon, the wind being at the south-west.

The last of October running west-south-west, about 24 leagues from Cape Frio, in Brazil, we fell with a great mountain which had a high round knop on the top of it standing from it like a town, with two little islands from it.

The first of November we went in between the island of St Sebastian and the mainland, and had our things on shore, and set up a forge, and had our cask on shore: our coopers made hoops, and so we remained there until the 23 day of the same month, in which time we fitted our things, built our pinnace, and filled our fresh water. And while our pinnace was in building there came a canoa from the river of Janeiro, meaning to go to St Vincent, wherein were six naked slaves of the country people, which did row the canoa, and one Portugal. And the Portugal knew Christopher Hare, master of the Admiral, for that Master Hare had been at St Vincent, in the *Minion* of London, in the year 1581. And thinking to have John Whithal, the Englishman which dwelleth at St Vincent, come unto us, which is twenty leagues from this harbour, with some other, thereby to have had some fresh victuals, we suffered the Portugal to go with a letter unto him, who promised to return or send some answer within ten days, for that we told him we were merchants, and would traffic with them. But we never received answer from him any more; and seeing that he came not according to appointment, our business being dispatched we weighed anchor, and set sail from St Sebastian on the 23 of November.

The 16 day of December we fell with the coast of

America in 47⅓ degrees, the land bearing west from us about 6 leagues off: from which place we ran along the shore, until we came into 48 degrees. It is a steep beach all along.

The 17 day of December in the afternoon we entered into a harbour, where our Admiral went in first: wherefore our General named the said harbour Port Desire. In which harbour is an island or two, where there is wonderful great store of seals, and another island of birds, which are grey gulls. These seals are of a wonderful great bigness, huge, and monstrous of shape, and for the fore-part of their bodies cannot be compared to anything better than to a lion: their head, and neck, and fore-parts of their bodies are full of rough hair: their feet are in manner of a fin, and in form like unto a man's hand: they breed every month, giving their young milk, yet continually get they their living in the sea, and live altogether upon fish: their young are marvellous good meat, and, being boiled or roasted, are hardly to be known from lamb or mutton. The old ones be of such bigness and force, that it is as much as 4 men are able to do to kill one of them with great cowl-staves: and he must be beaten down with striking on the head of him: for his body is of that bigness that four men could never kill him, but only on the head. For being shot through the body with an arquebus or a musket, yet he will go his way into the sea, and never care for it at the present. Also the fowls that were there, were very good meat, and great store of them: they have burrows in the ground like coneys, for they cannot fly. They have nothing but down upon their pinions: they also fish and feed in the sea for their living, and breed on shore.

Port Desire (Schouten's *Journael*)

This harbour is a very good place to trim ships in, and to bring them on ground, and grave them in, for there ebbeth and floweth much water: therefore we graved and trimmed all our ships there.

The 24 of December, being Christmas Even, a man and a boy of the Rear-admiral went some forty score from our ships into a very fair green valley at the foot of the mountains, where was a little pit or well which our men had digged and made some 2 or 3 days before to get fresh water, for there was none in all the harbour; and this was but brackish: therefore this man and boy came thither to wash their linen: and being in washing at the said well, there were great store of Indians which were come down, and found the said man and boy in washing. These Indians being divided on each side of the rocks, shot at them with their arrows and hurt them both, but they fled presently, being about fifty or threescore, though our General followed them but with 16 or 20 men. The man's name which was hurt was John Garge, the boy's name was Lutch: the man was shot clean through the knee, the boy into the shoulder, either of them having very sore wounds. Their arrows are made of little canes, and their heads are of a flint stone, set into the cane very artificially. They seldom or never see any Christians: they are as wild as ever was a buck or any other wild beast; for we followed them, and they ran from us as it had been the wildest thing in the world. We took the measure of one of their feet, and it was 18 inches long. Their use is when any of them die, to bring him or them to the cliffs by the sea-side, and upon the top of them they bury them, and in their graves are buried with them their bows and arrows, and all their jewels which they have in their lifetime, which are fine shells which they find by the sea-side, which they cut and square after an artificial manner: and all is laid under their heads. The grave is made all with great stones of great length and bigness, being set all along full of the dead man's darts which he used when he was living. And they colour both their darts and their graves with a red colour which they use in colouring of themselves.

The 28 of December we departed out of the Port of Desire, and went to an island which lieth 3 leagues to the southward of it; where we trimmed our saved penguins with salt for victual all that and the next day, and departed along the coast south-west and by south.

The 30 day we fell with a rock which lieth about 5 leagues from the land, much like unto Eddystone, which lieth off the sound of Plymouth, and we sounded, and had 8 fathoms rocky ground, within a mile thereof: the rock bearing west-south-west. We went coasting along south-south-west, and found great store of seals all along the coast. This rock standeth in 48½ degrees to the southward of the line.

The 2 day of January we fell with a very fair white cape, which standeth in 51 degrees, and had 7 fathoms water a league off the land.

The third day of the foresaid month we fell with another great white cape, which standeth in 52 degrees and 45 minutes: from which cape there runneth a low beach about a league to the southward, and this beach reacheth to the opening of the dangerous Strait of Magellan, which is in divers places 5 or 6 leagues wide, and in two several places more narrow. Under this cape we anchored and lost an anchor, for it was a great storm of foul weather, and lasted three days very dangerous.

The 6 day we put in for the Straits.

The 7 day between the mouth of the Straits and the narrowest place thereof, we took a Spaniard whose name was Hernando, who was there with 23 Spaniards more, which were all that remained of four hundred, which were left there three years before in these Straits of Magellan, all the rest being dead with famine. And the same day we passed through the narrowest of the Straits, where the aforesaid Spaniard showed us the hull of a small bark, which we judged to be a bark called the *John Thomas*. It is from the mouth of the Straits unto the narrowest of the Straits 14 leagues. and the course lieth west and by north. The mouth of the Straits standeth in 52 degrees.

From the narrowest of the Straits unto Penguin Island is 10 leagues, and lieth west-south-west somewhat to the southward, where we anchored the 8 day, and killed and salted great store of penguins for victuals.

The ninth day we departed from Penguin Island, and ran south-south-west to King Philip's City, which the Spaniards had built: which town or city had four forts, and every fort had in it one cast piece, which pieces were buried in the ground, the carriages were standing in their places unburied: we digged for them and had them all. They had contrived their city very well, and seated it in the best place of the Straits for wood and water: they had builded up their churches by themselves: they had laws very severe among themselves, for they had erected a gibbet, whereon they had done execution upon some of their company. It seemed unto us that their whole living for a great space was altogether upon mussels and limpets: for there was not anything else to be had, except some deer which came out of the mountains down to the fresh rivers to drink. These Spaniards which were there, were only come to fortify the Straits, to the end that no other nation should have passage through into the South Sea saving only their own: but as it appeared, it was not God's will so to have it. For during the time that they were there, which was two years at the least, they could never have anything to grow or in any wise prosper. And on the other side the Indians oftentimes preyed upon them, until their victuals grew so short (their store being spent which they had brought with them out of Spain, and having no means to renew the same), that they died like dogs in their houses, and in their clothes, wherein we found them still at our coming; until that in the end the town being wonderfully tainted with the smell and the savour of the dead people, the rest which remained alive were driven to bury such things as they had there in their town either for provision or for furniture, and so to forsake the town, and to go along the sea-side, and seek their victuals to preserve them from starving, taking nothing with them, but every man his arquebus and his furniture that was able to carry it (for some were not able to carry them for weakness) and so lived for the space of a year and more with roots, leaves, and sometimes a fowl which they might kill with their piece. To conclude, they were determined to have travelled towards the River of Plate, only being left alive 23 persons, whereof two were women, which were the remainder of 4 hundred. In this place we watered and wooded well and quietly. Our General named this town Port Famine: it standeth in 53 degrees by observation to the southward.

The 14 day we departed from this place, and ran south-south-west, and from thence south-west unto Cape Froward, 5 leagues west-south-west, which cape is the southermost part of all the straits, and standeth in the latitude of 54 degrees. From which cape we ran west and by north 5 leagues, and put into a bay or cove on the south side, which we called Mussel Cove, because there were great store of them : we rode therein 6 days, the wind being still westerly.

The 21 day of January we departed from Mussel Cove, and went north-west and by west 10 leagues to a very fair sandy bay on the north side, which our General called Elizabeth Bay, and as we rode there that night, one of our men died which went in the *Hugh Gallant*, whose name was Grey, a carpenter by his occupation, and was buried there in that bay.

The 22 we departed from Elizabeth Bay in the afternoon, and went about 2 leagues from that place, where there was a fresh-water river, where our General went up with the ship-boat about three miles. Which river hath very good and pleasant ground about it, and it is low and champaign soil, and so we saw none other ground else in all the Straits but that was craggy rocks and monstrous high hills and mountains. In this river are great store of savages, which we saw, and had conference with them. They were men-eaters, and fed altogether upon raw flesh, and other filthy food : which people had preyed upon some of the Spaniards before spoken of. For they had gotten knives and pieces of rapiers to make darts of. They used all the means they could possibly to have allured us up farther into the river, of purpose to have betrayed us ; which being espied by our General, he caused us to shoot at them with our arquebuses, whereby we killed many of them. So we sailed from this river to the Channel of St Jerome, which is 2 leagues off.

From the river of St Jerome about three or four leagues, we ran west unto a cape which is on the north side : and from that cape unto the mouth of the Straits the course lieth north-west and by west, and north-west. Between which place and the mouth of the Straits to the southward we lay in harbour until the three and twentieth of February, by reason of contrary winds and most vile and filthy foul weather, with such rain and vehement stormy winds which came down from the mountains and high hills, that they hazarded the best cables and anchors that we had for to hold, which if they had failed, we had been in great danger to have been cast away, or at the least famished. For during this time, which was a full month, we fed almost altogether upon mussels and limpets, and birds, or such as we could get on shore, seeking every day for them, as the fowls of the air do, where they can find food, in continual rainy weather.

There is at every mile or two miles' end a harbour on both sides of the land. And there are between the river of St Jerome and the mouth of the Straits going into the South Sea about 34 leagues by estimation. So that the length of the whole Straits is about 90 leagues. And the said mouth of the Straits standeth in the same height that the entrance standeth in when we pass out of the North Sea, which is about 52 degrees and $\frac{2}{3}$ to the southward of the line.

The 24 day of February we entered into the South Sea : and on the south side of the going out of the Straits is a fair high cape with a low point adjoining unto it; and on the north side are 4 or 5 islands, which lie 6 leagues off the main, and much broken and sunken ground about them. By noon the same day we had brought these islands east of us 5 leagues off; the wind being southerly.

The first of March a storm took us at north, which night the ships lost the company of the *Hugh Gallant*, being in 49½ and 45 leagues from the land. This storm continued 3 or 4 days, and for that time we in the *Hugh Gallant* being separated from the other 2 ships, looked every hour to sink, our bark was so leak, and ourselves so dilvered and weakened with freeing it of water, that we slept not in three days and three nights.

The 15 of March in the morning the *Hugh Gallant* came in between the Island of St Mary and the main, where she met with the Admiral and the *Content*, which had rid at the island called La Mocha 2 days, which standeth in the southerly latitude of 38 degrees: at which place some of our men went on shore with the Vice-admiral's boat, where the Indians fought with them with their bows and arrows, and were marvellous wary of their calivers. These Indians were enemies to the Spaniards, and belonged to a great place called Arauco, and took us for Spaniards, as afterward we learned.

This place which is called Arauco is wonderful rich, and full of gold mines, and yet could it not be subdued at any time by the Spaniards, but they always returned with the greatest loss of men. For these Indians are marvellous desperate and careless of their lives to live at their own liberty and freedom.

The 15 day aforesaid in the afternoon we weighed anchor, and ran under the west side of Saint Mary

Island, where we rid very well in 6 fathoms water, and very-fair ground all that night.

The 16 day our General went on shore himself with 70 or 80 men, every one with his furniture. There came down to us certain Indians with two which were the principals of the island to welcome us on shore, thinking we had been Spaniards, for it is subdued by them; who brought us up to a place where the Spaniards had erected a church with crosses and altars in it. And there were about this church 2 or 3 storehouses, which were full of wheat and barley ready threshed and made up in cades of straw to the quantity of a bushel of corn in every cade. The wheat and barley was as fair, as clean, and everyway as good as any we have in England. There were also the like cades full of potato roots, which were very good to eat, ready made up in the storehouses for the Spaniards against they should come for their tribute. This island also yieldeth many sorts of fruits, hogs, and hens. These Indians are held in such slavery by them, that they dare not eat a hen or a hog themselves. But the Spaniards have made them all in that island Christians. Thus we fitted ourselves here with corn as much as we would have, and as many hogs as we had salt to powder them withal, and great store of hens, with a number of bags of potato roots, and about 500 dried dog-fish, and Guinea wheat, which is called maize. And having taken as much as we would have, yet we left marvellous great store behind us. Our General had the two principals of the island aboard our ship, and provided great cheer for them, and made them merry with wine: and they in the end perceiving us to be no Spaniards, made signs, as near as our General could perceive, that if we would go over unto

the mainland unto Arauco, that there was much gold,
making us signs, that we should have great store of
riches. But because we could not understand them,
our General made some haste, and within 2 or three
days we furnished ourselves.

The 18 day in the morning we departed from this
place, and ran all that day north-north-east about 10
leagues, and at night lay with a short sail off and on
the coast.

The 19 we ran in east-north-east with the land,
and bare in with a place called The Conception, where
we anchored under an island, and departed the next
morning without going on land.

The 20 we departed from The Conception, and went
into a little bay which was sandy, where we saw fresh
water and cattle, but we stayed not there.

The 30 day we came into the Bay of Quintero, which
standeth in 33 degrees and 50 minutes.

The said day, presently after we were come unto an
anchor in the bay, there was a neatherd, or one that
kept cattle, which lay upon the point of the hill asleep,
which when he awaked and had espied three ships
which were come into the bay, before we could get on
shore, he had caught a horse which was feeding by,
and rode his way as fast as ever he might: and our
General with 30 shot with him went on shore. He had
not been on land one hour, but there came 3 horsemen
with bright swords towards us so hard as they might
ride, until they came within some twenty or thirty
score of us, and so stayed, and would come no nearer
unto us. So our General sent unto them a couple of
our men with their shot, and one Fernando, which was
the Spaniard that we had taken up at the mouth of the

Straits, which was one of the 400 that were starved there. But the Spaniards would not suffer our men to come near with their shot, but made signs that one of our men should come alone unto them: so the said Fernando the Spaniard went unto them, and our two men stood not far from them. They had great conference, and in the end Fernando came back from them, and told our General that he had parleyed with them for some victuals, who had promised as much as we would have. Our General sent him back again with another message and another shot with him: and being come near unto them, they would not suffer any more than one to approach them; whereupon our men let the Spaniard go unto them alone himself, who being some good distance from them, they stayed but a small time together, but that the said Fernando leaped up behind one of them and rid away with them, for all his deep and damnable oaths which he had made continually to our General and all his company never to forsake him, but to die on his side before he would be false. Our General, seeing how he was dealt withal, filled water all that day with good watch, and carried it aboard: and night being come, he determined the next day to send into the country to find their town, and to have taken the spoil of it, and to have fired it if they could have found it.

The last of March Captain Havers went up into the country with 50 or 60 men with their shot and furniture with them, and we travelled 7 or 8 miles into the land; and as we were marching along, we espied a number of herds of cattle, of kine and bullocks, which were wonderful wild. We saw also great store of horses, mares, and colts, which were very wild and unhandled. There is also great store of hares and coneys, and plenty of partridges and other wild fowls. The country is very fruitful, with fair fresh rivers all along full of wild fowl of all sorts. Having travelled so far that we could go no further for the monstrous high mountains, we rested ourselves at a very fair fresh river running in and along fair low meadows at the foot of the mountains, where every man drank of the river, and refreshed themselves. Having so done, we returned to our ships the likest way that we thought their town should be. So we travelled all the day long, not seeing any man, but we met with many wild dogs: yet there were two hundred horsemen abroad that same day by means of the Spaniard which they had taken the day before from us, who had told them that our force was but small, and that we were wonderfully weak; who though they did espy us that day, yet durst they not give the onset upon us. For we marched along in array, and observed good order, whereby we seemed a great number more than we were, until we came unto our ships that night again.

The next day, being the first of April 1587, our men went on shore to fill water at a pit which was a quarter of a mile from the water's side: and being early hard at their business were in no readiness. In which mean while there came pouring down from the hills almost 200 horsemen, and before our people could return to the rocks from the watering-place, twelve of them were cut off, part killed, and part taken prisoners; the rest were rescued by our soldiers which came from the rocks to meet with them, who being but fifteen of us that had any weapons on shore, yet we made the enemy retire in the end with loss of some four and twenty of their men, after we had skirmished with them an hour.

The names of our men that were slain were these:—

Thomas Lucas of London, soldier.
Richard Wheeler of London.
Robert Pitcher of Norfolk, soldier.
John Langston of Gloucestershire.
William Kingman of Dorsetshire, soldier.
William Hills of Cornwall.

Out of the Admiral.

1 William Byet of Weymouth.
2 Laurence Gamesby of Newcastle.

Killed out of the Vice-adm.

1 Henry Blackenals of Weymouth.
2 William Stevens of Plymouth, gunner.
3 William Pitt of Sherborne, in Dorsetshire.
4 Humphrey Derrick of London.

Killed out of the *Hugh Gallant.*

After the loss of these men, we rid in the road, and watered in despite of them with good watch and ward, until the fifth of the said month.

The fifth day we departed out of this bay of Quintero: and off from the bay there lieth a little island about a league distant, whereon there are great store of penguins and other fowls; whereof we took to serve our turns, and sailed away north, and north and by west: for so lieth the coast along in this place.

The fifteenth we came thwart of a place which is called Morro Moreno, which standeth in 23½ degrees, and is an excellent good harbour; and there is an island which maketh it a harbour, and a ship may go in at either end of the island. Here we went with our General on shore to the number of 30 men: and at our going on shore upon our landing, the Indians of the place came down from the rocks to meet with us, with fresh water and wood on their backs. They are in marvellous awe

of the Spaniards, and very simple people, and live marvellous savagely. For they brought us to their bidings
about two miles from the harbour, where we saw their
women and lodging, which is nothing but the skin of some
beast laid upon the ground: and over them, instead of
houses, is nothing but five or six sticks laid across,
which stand upon two forks with sticks on the ground
and a few boughs laid on it. Their diet is raw fish,
which stinketh most vilely. And when any of them
die, they bury their bows and arrows with them, with
their canoa and all that they have; for we opened one
of their graves, and saw the order of them. Their
canoas or boats are marvellous artificially made of two
skins like unto bladders, and blown full at one end
with quills. They have two of these bladders blown
full, which are sewn together and made fast with a
sinew of some wild beast; which when they are in the
water swell, so that they are as tight as may be. They
go to sea in these boats, and catch very much fish with
them, and pay much of it for tribute unto the Spaniards:
but they use it marvellous beastly.

The 23 in the morning we took a small bark which
came out of Arica road, which we kept and called the
George: the men forsook it, and went away with their
boat. Our Admiral's pinnace followed the boat, and
the *Hugh Gallant's* boat took the bark. Our Admiral's
pinnace could not recover the boat before it got on
shore, but went along into the road of Arica, and laid
aboard a great ship of an hundred tons riding in the
road right afore the town, but all the men and goods
were gone out of it, only the bare ship was left alone.
They made three or four very fair shots at the pinnace
as she was coming in, but missed her very narrowly

with a minion shot which they had in the fort. Whereupon we came into the road with the Admiral and the *Hugh Gallant*; but the *Content*, which was Vice-admiral, was behind out of sight: by means whereof, and for want of her boat to land men withal, we landed not; otherwise if we had been together, our General with the company would resolutely have landed to take the town, whatsoever had come of it. The cause why the *Content* stayed behind was, that she had found about 14 leagues to the southward of Arica, in a place where the Spaniards had landed, a whole ship's lading of botijas of wine of Castilia, whereof the said *Content* took into her as many as she could conveniently carry, and came after us into the road of Arica the same day. By this time we perceived that the town had gathered all their power together, and also conveyed all their treasure away, and buried it before we were come near the town: for they had heard of us. Now because it was very populous with the aid of one or two places up in the land, our General saw there was no landing without loss of many men: wherefore he gave over that enterprise. While we rid in the road they shot at us, and our ships shot at them again for every shot two. Moreover, our pinnace went in hard almost to the shore, and fetched out another bark which rid there, in despite of all their forts, though they shot still at the pinnace, which they could never hit. After these things our General sent a boat on shore with a flag of truce to know if they would redeem their great ship or no; but they would not: for they had received special commandment from the Viceroy from Lima, not to buy any ship, nor to ransom any man upon pain of death. Our General did this in hope to have redeemed some of our men, which were taken prisoners on shore by the horsemen at Quintero, otherwise he would have made them no offer of parley.

The 25, riding still in the said road, we spied a sail coming from the southward, and our General sent out his pinnace to meet her, with all our boats; but the town made such signs from the hill with fires and tokens out of the watch-house, that before our pinnace could get to them, they ran the bark on shore two miles to the southward of the town; but they had small leisure to carry anything with them. But all the men scaped; among whom there were certain friars, for we saw them in their friars' weeds as they ran on shore: many horsemen came from the town to rescue them, and to carry them away, otherwise we had landed and taken or killed them. So we went aboard the bark as she lay sunk, and fetched out the pillage: but there was nothing in it of any value, and came aboard our ships again the same night. And the next morning we set the great ship on fire in the road, and sunk one of the barks, and carried the other along with us, and so departed from thence, and went away north-west.

The 27 day we took a small bark, which came from St Iago, near unto Quintero, where we lost our men first. In this bark was one George, a Greek, a reasonable pilot for all the coast of Chili. They were sent to the city of Lima with letters of adviso of us, and of the loss of our men. There were also in the said bark one Fleming and three Spaniards, and they were all sworn and received the Sacrament before they came to sea by three or four friars, that if we should chance to meet them, they should throw those letters overboard: which (as we were giving them chase with our pinnace), before we could fetch them up, they had accordingly thrown away. Yet our General wrought so with them, that they did confess it: but he was fain to cause them to be tormented with their thumbs in a wrench, and to continue them at several times with extreme pain. Also he made the old Fleming believe that he would hang him; and the rope being about his neck he was pulled up a little from the hatches, and yet he would not confess, choosing rather to die, than he would be perjured. In the end it was confessed by one of the Spaniards; whereupon we burnt the bark, and carried the men with us.

The third of May we came into a bay where are three little towns, which are called Paracca, Chincha, and Pisca, where some of us landed and took certain houses, wherein was bread, wine, figs, and hens: but the sea went so high, that we could not land at the best of the towns without sinking of our boats, and great hazard of us all. This place standeth in thirteen degrees and $\frac{2}{3}$ to the southward of the line.

The fifth of May we departed from this harbour, leaving the *Content*, our Vice-admiral, within at an island of seals, by which means at that time we lost her company.

The ninth we gave chase to a sail, namely, our Admiral, the *Hugh Gallant*, and the *George*, which we had taken before coming out of the road of Arica; the *Content*, which was our Vice-admiral, being still lost: but we could not fetch it. The *George* made after it, but lost it that night.

The tenth day the *Hugh Gallant* (in which bark I Francis Pretty was) lost company of our Admiral.

The eleventh we which were in the *Hugh Gallant* put

into a bay which standeth in 12⅔ degrees, in which bay
we found a river of fresh water about eight of the clock
at night; and though we were but of small force, and
no more but one bark and 18 men in it, yet we went
on shore to fill water; where having filled one boat's
lading, while our boat was in going aboard, two or
three of our company which were on shore, as they
were going a little from the watering-place with their
furniture about them, espied where there were four or
five hundred bags of meal on a heap covered with
a few reeds. So that night we filled water and took
as much meal as we thought good: which fell out well
for us that were then lost and stood in need of victuals;
and by break of day in the morning we came aboard,
and there stayed and rode until the afternoon. In which
mean time the town seeing us ride there still, brought
down much cattle to the sea side to have enticed us to
come on shore: but we saw their intent, and weighed
anchor and departed the twelfth day.

The 13 day at night we put into a bay which standeth
in 9 degrees and ⅓, where we saw horsemen: and that
night we landed, namely, Master Brewer, captain,
myself Francis Pretty, Arthur Warford, John Way,
Preacher, John Newman, Andrew Wight, William
Gargefield, and Henry Hilliard. And we 8 only,
having every man his arquebus and his furniture
about him, marched three-quarters of a mile along the
sea side, where we found a boat of five or six tons
haled up dry on the shore about a cable's length from
the water; and with extreme labour we launched the
bark. When it was on float, Captain Brewer and I went
in, while the rest of our company were fetching their
things: but suddenly it was ready to sink. And the

captain and I stood up to the knees lading out water with our targets; but it sunk down faster than we were able to free it, insomuch as in the end we had much ado to save ourselves from drowning. When we were out, we stood in great fear that our own boat wherein we came on shore was sunk: for we could nowhere see it. Howbeit the captain commanded them to keep it off, for fear of the great surge that went by the shore. Yet in the end we spied it, and went aboard by two and two, and were driven to wade up to the arm-holes 60 paces into the sea before we could get into the boat, by reason of the shoalness: and then departed the fourteenth day in the morning.

The 16 we took with the *Hugh Gallant*, being but sixteen men of us in it, a great ship which came from Guaiaquil, which was called the *Lewis*, and was of the burthen of three hundred tons, having four and twenty men in it, wherein was pilot one Gonsalvo de Ribas, whom we carried along with us, and a negro called Emmanuel. The ship was laden with nothing but timber and victuals: wherefore we left her seven leagues from the land very leak and ready to sink in 7 degrees to the southward of the line: we sank her boat and took away her foresail and certain victuals.

The 17 of May we met with our Admiral again, and all the rest of our fleet. They had taken two ships, the one laden with sugar, molasses, maize, Cordovan-skins, manteca de puerco, many packs of pintados, many Indian coats, and some marmalade, and 1000 hens: and the other ship was laden with wheat-meal, and boxes of marmalade. One of these ships which had the chief merchandise in it, was worth twenty thousand pounds, if it had been in England or in any other place of Christendom where we might have sold it.   We filled all our ships with as much as we could bestow of these goods: the rest we burnt and the ships also; and set the men and women that were not killed on shore.

The 20 day in the morning we came into the road of Paita, and being at an anchor, our General landed with sixty or seventy men, skirmished with them of the town, and drave them all to flight to the top of the hill which is over the town, except a few slaves and some other which were of the meaner sort, who were commanded by the governors to stay below in the town, at a place which is in building for a fort, having with them a bloody ensign, being in number about one hundred men. Now as we were rowing between the ships and the shore, our gunner shot off a great piece out of one of the barks, and the shot fell among them, and drave them to fly from the fort as fast as they might run; who got them up upon a hill, and from thence shot among us with their small shot.   After we were landed and had taken the town, we ran upon them, and chased them so fiercely up the hills for the space of an hour that we drave them in the end away perforce, and being got up the hills, we found where they had laid all their stuff which they had brought out of the town, and had hidden it there upon the mountains.   We also found the quantity of 25 pounds weight in silver in pieces of eight reals, and abundance of household stuff and storehouses full of all kind of wares.   But our General would not suffer any man to carry much cloth or apparel away, because they should not cloy themselves with burdens: for he knew not whether our enemies were provided with furniture according to the number of their men; for they were five men to one of us, and we had an English mile and a half to our ships. Thus we came down in safety to the town, which was very well builded, and marvellous clean kept in every street, with a town-house or Guildhall in the midst, and had to the number of two hundred houses at the least in it. We set it on fire to the ground, and goods to the value of five or six thousand pounds: there was also a bark riding in the road which we set on fire, and departed, directing our course to the Island of Puna.

The 25 day of May we arrived at the Island of Puna, where is a very good harbour, where we found a great ship of the burthen of 250 tons riding at an anchor with all her furniture, which was ready to be haled on ground: for there is a special good place for that purpose. We sunk it, and went on shore where the lord of the island dwelt, which was by the water's side, who had a sumptuous house, marvellous well contrived, with very many singular good rooms and chambers in it: and out of every chamber was framed a gallery with a stately prospect into the sea on the one side, and into the island on the other side, with a marvellous great hall below, and a very great storehouse at the one end of the hall, which was filled with botijas of pitch, and bash to make cables withal; for the most part of the cables in the South Sea are made upon that island. This great cacique doth make all the Indians upon the island to work and to drudge for him: and he himself is an Indian born, but is married to a marvellous fair woman which is a Spaniard, by reason of his pleasant habitation and of his great wealth.

This Spanish woman his wife is honoured as a queen in the island, and never goeth on the ground upon her feet, but holdeth it too base a thing for her. But when her pleasure is to take the air, or to go abroad, she is always carried in a shadow like unto a horse-litter upon four men's shoulders, with a veil or canopy over her for the sun or the wind, having her gentlewomen still attending about her, with a great troop of the best men of the island with her. But both she and the lord of the island with all the Indians in the town were newly fled out of the island before we could get to an anchor, by reason we were becalmed before we could get in, and were gone over unto the mainland, having carried away with them to the sum of 100,000 crowns, which we knew by a captain of the island, an Indian, which was left there with some other upon the island under him, whom we had taken at sea as we were coming into the road, being in a balsa or canoa for a spy to see what we were.

The 27 our General himself with certain shot and some targeteers went over into the main unto the place where this aforesaid Indian captain which we had taken had told us that the cacique, which was the lord of all the island, was gone unto, and had carried all his treasure with him: but at our coming to the place which we went to land at, we found newly arrived there four or five great balsas, which were laden with plantains, bags of meal, and many other kinds of victuals. Our General marvelled what they were and what they meant, asking the Indian guide and commanding him to speak the truth upon his life: being then bound fast, he answered, being very much abashed, as well as our company were, that he neither knew from whence they should come, nor who they should be; for there was never a man in any one of the balsas; and

because he had told our General before, that it was
an easy matter to take the said cacique and all his
treasure, and that there were but three or four houses
standing in a desert place and no resistance, and that
if he found it not so, he should hang him.   Again being
demanded to speak upon his life what he thought these
balsas should be, he answered that he could not say
from whence they should come, except it were to bring
60 soldiers, which he did hear were to go to a place
called Guaiaquil, which was about 6 leagues from the
said island, where two or three of the king's ships were
on the stocks in building, where are continually an
hundred soldiers in garrisons who had heard of us, and
had sent for sixty more for fear of burning of the ships
and town.   Our General not any whit discouraged either
at the sight of the balsas unlooked for, or for hearing of
the threescore soldiers not until then spoken of, with
a brave courage animating his company in the exploit,
went presently forward, being in the night in a most
desert path in the woods, until such time as he came
to the place; where, as it seemed, they had kept watch
either at the water's side, or at the houses, or else at
both, and were newly gone out of the houses, having
so short warning, that they left the meat both boiling
and roasting at the fire, and were fled with their treasure
with them, or else buried it where it could not be found,
being also in the night.   Our company took hens and
such things as we thought good, and came away.

The 29 day of May our General went in the ship-
boat into a little island thereby, whereas the said
cacique which was the lord of Puna had caused all
the hangings of his chambers, which were of Cordovan
leather all gilded over, and painted very fair and rich,

with all his household stuff, and all the ship's tackling which was riding in the road at our coming in, with great store of nails, spikes of iron, and very many other things, to be conveyed: all which we found, and brought away what our General thought requisite for the ship's business.

This island is very pleasant for all things requisite, and fruitful: but there are no mines of gold or silver in it. There are at the least 200 houses in the town about the cacique's palace, and as many in one or two towns more upon the island, which is almost as big as the Isle of Wight, in England. There is planted on the one side of the cacique's house a fair garden, with all herbs growing in it, and at the lower end a well of fresh water, and round about it are trees set, whereon bombasin cotton groweth after this manner. The tops of the trees grow full of cods, out of which the cotton groweth, and in the cotton is a seed of the bigness of a pea, and in every cod there are seven or eight of these seeds: and if the cotton be not gathered when it is ripe, then these seeds fall from it, and spring again.

There are also in this garden fig-trees which bear continually, also pompions, melons, cucumbers, radishes, rosemary, and thyme, with many other herbs and fruits. At the other end of the house there is also another orchard, where grow oranges sweet and sour, lemons, pomegranates, and limes, with divers other fruits.

There is very good pasture ground in this island; and withal many horses, oxen, bullocks, sheep very fat and fair, great store of goats which be very tame, and are used continually to be milked. They have moreover abundance of pigeons, turkeys, and ducks of a marvellous bigness.

There was also a very large and great church hard by the cacique's house, whither he caused all the Indians in the island to come and hear mass : for he himself was made a Christian when he was married to the Spanish woman before spoken of, and upon his conversion he caused the rest of his subjects to be christened. In this church was a high altar with a crucifix, and five bells hanging in the nether end thereof. We burnt the church and brought the bells away.

By this time we had haled on ground our Admiral, and had made her clean, burnt her keel, pitched and tarred her, and had haled her on float again ; and in the meanwhile continually kept watch and ward in the great house both night and day.

The second day of June in the morning, by-and-by after break of day, every one of the watch being gone abroad to seek to fetch in victuals, some one way, some another, some for hens, some for sheep, some for goats, upon the sudden there came down upon us a hundred Spanish soldiers with muskets and an ensign, which were landed on the other side of the island that night, and all the Indians of the island with them, every one with weapons and their baggage after them : which was by means of a negro, whose name was Emmanuel, which fled from us at our first landing there. Thus being taken at advantage we had the worst ; for our company was not past sixteen or twenty ; whereof they had slain one or two before they were come to the houses. Yet we skirmished with them an hour and a half : at the last, being sore overcharged with multitudes, we were driven down from the hill to the water's side, and there kept them play awhile, until in the end Zachary Saxie, who with his halberd had kept the way of the hill, and slain a couple of them, as he breathed himself, being somewhat tired, had an honourable death and a short; for a shot struck him to the heart; who feeling himself mortally wounded, cried to God for mercy, and fell down presently dead. But soon after the enemy was driven somewhat to retire from the bank's side to the green: and in the end our boat came and carried as many of our men away as could go in her, which was in hazard of sinking while they hastened into it. And one of our men, whose name was Robert Maddock, was shot through the head with his own piece, being a snap-hance, as he was hasting into the boat. But four of us were left behind which the boat could not carry: to wit, myself Francis Pretty, Thomas Andrews, Stephen Gunner, and Richard Rose; which had our shot ready and retired ourselves unto a cliff, until the boat came again, which was presently after they had carried the rest aboard. There were six and forty of the enemy slain by us, whereof they had dragged some into bushes, and some into old houses, which we found afterward. We lost twelve men, in manner following:—

1 Zachary Saxie,
2 Neales Johnson,
3 William Gargefield, } Slain by the enemy.
4 Nicholas Hendy,
5 Henry Cooper,

1 Robert Maddock, killed with his piece.
2 Henry Mawdly, burnt.

1 Edward, the gunner's man, } drowned.
2 Ambrose, the musician,

1 Walter Tilliard, ⎫
2 Edward Smith, ⎬ taken prisoners.
3 Henry Aselye, ⎭

The self-same day being the second of June, we went on shore again with seventy men, and had a fresh skirmish with the enemy, and drave them to retire, being a hundred Spaniards serving with muskets, and two hundred Indians with bows, arrows, and darts. This done, we set fire on the town and burnt it to the ground, having in it to the number of three hundred houses: and shortly after made havoc of their fields, orchards, and gardens, and burnt four great ships more which were in building on the stocks.

The third of June, the *Content*, which was our Vice-admiral, was haled on ground, to grave at the same place in despite of the Spaniards, and also our pinnace, which the Spaniards had burned, was new trimmed.

The fifth day of June we departed out of the road of Puna, where we had remained eleven days, and turned up for a place which is called Rio Dolce, where we watered: at which place also we sunk our Rear-admiral called the *Hugh Gallant*, for want of men, being a bark of forty tons.

The tenth day of the same month we set the Indians on shore, which we had taken before in a balsa as we were coming into the road of Puna.

The eleventh day we departed from the said Rio Dolce.

The twelfth of June we doubled the equinoctial line, and continued our course northward all that month.

The first of July we had sight of the coast of Nueva España, being four leagues distant from land in the latitude of ten degrees to the northward of the line.

The ninth of July we took a new ship of the burthen of 120 tons, wherein was one Michael Sancius, whom our General took to serve his turn to water along the coast: for he was one of the best coasters in the South Sea. This Michael Sancius was a Provençal, born in Marseilles, and was the first man that told us news of the great ship called the *Santa Anna*, which we afterward took coming from the Philippinas.

There were six men more in this new ship: we took her sails, her ropes, and firewood, to serve our turns, set her on fire, and kept the men.

The tenth we took another bark which was going with advice of us and our ships all along the coast, as Michael Sancius told us: but all the company that were in the bark were fled on shore. None of both these ships had any goods in them. For they came both from Sonsonate in the province of Guatemala; the new ship, for fear we should have taken her in the road, and the bark, to carry news of us along the coast; which bark also we set on fire.

The 26 day of July we came to an anchor at 10 fathoms in the river of Copalita, where we made account to water. And the same night we departed with 30 men in the pinnace, and rowed to Aguatulco, which is but two leagues from the aforesaid river; and standeth in 15 degrees 40 minutes to the northward of the equinoctial line.

The 27 in the morning by the break of day we came into the road of Aguatulco, where we found a bark of 50 tons, which was come from Sonsonate laden with cacaos and anil, which they had there landed: and the men were all fled on shore. We landed there, and burnt their town, with the church and custom-house, which was very fair and large: in which house were 600 bags of anil to dye cloth, every bag whereof was worth 40 crowns; and 400 bags of cacaos, every bag whereof is worth ten crowns. These cacaos go among them for meat and money. For 150 of them are in value one real of plate in ready payment. They are very like unto an almond, but are nothing so pleasant in taste: they eat them, and make drink of them. This the owner of the ship told us. I found in this town, before we burnt it, a flasket full of boxes of balm. After we had spoiled and burnt the town, wherein there were some hundred houses, the owner of the ship came down out of the hills with a flag of truce unto us, which before with the rest of all the townsmen was run away at our first coming; and at length came aboard our pinnace upon Captain Havers' word of safe return. We carried him to the river of Copalita where our ships rode: and when he came to our General, he caused him to be set on shore in safety the same night, because he came upon the captain's word.

The 28 day we set sail from Copalita, because the sea was so great there, that we could not fill water, and ran the same night into the road of Aguatulco.

The 29 our General landed and went on shore with thirty men two miles into the woods, where we took a mestizo, whose name was Michael de Truxillo, who was Customer of that town, and we found with him two chambers full of his stuff: we brought him and his stuff aboard. And whereas I say he was a mestizo, it is to be understood that a mestizo is one which hath a Spaniard to his father and an Indian to his mother.

The second day of August, we had watered, and examined the said mestizo, and set him on shore again and departed from the port of Aguatulco the same night, which standeth, as I said before, in 15 degrees and 40 minutes to the northward of the line.

Here we overslipped the haven of Acapulco, from whence the ships are set forth for the Philippinas.

The four and twentieth day of August, our General, with 30 of us, went with the pinnace unto an haven called Puerto de Natividad, where we had intelligence by Michael Sancius that there should be a pinnace, but before we could get thither the said pinnace was gone to fish for pearls 12 leagues farther, as we were informed by certain Indians which we found there. We took a mulatto in this place, in his bed, which was sent with letters of advice concerning us along the coast of Nueva Galicia; whose horse we killed, took his letters, left him behind, set fire on the houses, and burnt two new ships of 200 tons the piece, which were in building there on the stocks, and came aboard of our ships again.

The six and twenty day of August, we came into the bay of St Iago, where we watered at a fresh river, along which river many plantains are growing. Here is great abundance of fresh fish. Here also certain of our company dragged for pearls and caught some quantity.

The second of September we departed from St Iago at four of the clock in the evening. This bay of St Iago standeth in nineteen degrees and eighteen minutes to the northward of the line.

The 3 of September we arrived in a little bay a league to the westward of Port de Natividad, called Malacca, which is a very good place to ride in: and the same day about twelve of the clock our General landed with thirty men or thereabout, and went up to a town of Indians which was two leagues from the road, which town is called Acatlan. There were in it about 20 or 30 houses and a church, which we defaced, and came aboard again the same night. All the people were fled out of the town at the sight of us.

The fourth of September, we departed from the road of Malacca, and sailed along the coast.

The 8 we came to the road of Chaccalla, in which bay there are two little houses by the water's side. This bay is 18 leagues from the Cape de los Corrientes.

The 9 in the morning our General sent up Captain Havers with forty men of us before day, and Michael Sancius being our guide, we went unto a place about two leagues up into the country in a most villainous desert path through the woods and wilderness: and in the end we came to a place where we took three householders with their wives and children and some Indians, one carpenter, which was a Spaniard, and a Portugal; we bound them all and made them to come to the sea-side with us.

Our General made their wives to fetch us plantains, lemons, and oranges, pineapples, and other fruits, whereof they had abundance, and so let their husbands depart, except Sembrano, the Spanish carpenter, and Diego, the Portugal; and the tenth day we departed the road.

The twelfth day we arrived at a little island called the Isle of Saint Andrew, on which there is great store of fowl and wood, where we dried and salted as many of the fowls as we thought good. We also killed there abundance of seals and iguanas, which are a kind of serpent, with four feet, and a long sharp tail, strange to them which have not seen them; but they are very

11—2

good meat. We rid here until the seventeenth day, at which time we departed.

The 24 day we arrived in the road of Mazatlan, which standeth in 23½ degrees, just under the Tropic of Cancer. It is a very great river within, but it is barred at the mouth: and upon the north side of the bar without, is good fresh water: but there is very evil filling of it; because at a low water it is shoal half a mile off the shore. There is great store of fresh fish in that bay, and good fruits up into the country, whereof we had some, though not without danger.

The seven and twentieth day of September, we departed from the road of Mazatlan and ran to an island which is a league to the northward the said Mazatlan, where we trimmed our ships and new built our pinnace: and there is a little island a quarter of a league from it, on which are seals, where a Spanish prisoner, whose name was Domingo, being sent to wash shirts with one of our men to keep him, made a scape, and swam to the main, which was an English mile distant: at which place we had seen 30 or 40 Spaniards and Indians, which were horsemen, and kept watch there, which came from a town called Chiametla, which was 11 leagues up into the country, as Michael Sancius told us. We found upon the island where we trimmed our pinnace fresh water, by the assistance of God in that our great need, by digging two or three foot deep in the sand, where no water nor sign of water was before to be perceived. Otherwise we had gone back 20 or 30 leagues to water, which might have been occasion that we might have missed our prey we had long waited for. But God raised one Flores, a Spaniard, which was also a prisoner with us, to make a motion to dig in the sands. Now our General having had experience once before of the like, commanded to put his motion in practice, and in digging three foot deep we found very good and fresh water. So we watered our ships, and might have filled a thousand tuns more, if we had would.

We stayed in this island until the 9 day of October, at which time we departed at night for the Cape of St Lucar, which is on the west side of the point of California.

The 14 of October we fell with the Cape of St Lucar, which cape is very like the Needles at the Isle of Wight; and within the said cape is a great bay called by the Spaniards Aguada Segura : into which bay falleth a fair fresh river, about which many Indians use to keep. We watered in the river, and lay off and on from the said Cape of St Lucar until the fourth of November, and had the winds hanging still westerly.

The 4 of November the *Desire* and the *Content*, wherein were the number of [1] Englishmen only living, beating up and down upon the headland of California, which standeth in 23 degrees and $\frac{2}{3}$ to the northward, between seven and 8 of the clock in the morning one of the company of our Admiral, which was the trumpeter of the ship, going up into the top, espied a sail bearing in from the sea with the cape. Whereupon he cried out, with no small joy to himself and the whole company, "A sail! a sail!" With which cheerful word the master of the ship and divers others of the company went also up into the maintop. Who, perceiving the speech to be very true, gave information unto our General of these happy news, who was no less glad than the cause required : whereupon he gave in charge presently unto

1 Blank in the original.

the whole company to put all things in readiness. Which being performed we gave them chase some 3 or 4 hours, standing with our best advantage and working for the wind. In the afternoon we gat up unto them, giving them the broadside with our great ordnance and a volley of small shot, and presently laid the ship aboard, whereof the king of Spain was owner, which was Admiral of the South Sea, called the *St Anna*, and thought to be 700 tons in burthen. Now, as we were ready on their ship's side to enter her, being not past 50 or 60 men at the uttermost in our ship, we perceived that the captain of the said ship had made fights fore and after, and laid their sails close on their poop, their midship, with their forecastle, and having not one man to be seen, stood close under their fights, with lances, javelins, rapiers, and targets, and an innumerable sort of great stones, which they threw overboard upon our heads and into our ship so fast, and being so many of them, that they put us off the ship again, with the loss of 2 of our men which were slain, and with the hurting of 4 or 5. But for all this we new trimmed our sails, and fitted every man his furniture, and gave them a fresh encounter with our great ordnance and also with our small shot, raking them through and through, to the killing and maiming of many of their men. Their captain still, like a valiant man, with his company, stood very stoutly unto his close fights, not yielding as yet. Our General, encouraging his men afresh with the whole noise of trumpets, gave them the third encounter with our great ordnance and all our small shot, to the great discomforting of our enemies, raking them through in divers places, killing and spoiling many of their men. They being thus discomforted and spoiled, and their ship being in hazard of sinking by reason of the great shot which were made, whereof some were under water, within 5 or 6 hours' fight set out a flag of truce and parleyed for mercy, desiring our General to save their lives and to take their goods, and that they would presently yield. Our General of his goodness promised them mercy, and willed them to strike their sails, and to hoise out their boat and to come aboard. Which news they were full glad to hear of, and presently struck their sails, hoised their boat out, and one of their chief merchants came aboard unto our General, and falling down upon his knees, offered to have kissed our General's feet, and craved mercy. Our General most graciously pardoned both him and the rest upon promise of their true dealing with him and his company concerning such riches as were in the ship: and sent for the captain and their pilot, who at their coming used the like duty and reverence as the former did. The General, of his great mercy and humanity, promised their lives and good usage. The said captain and pilot presently certified the General what goods they had within board, to wit, an hundred and 22 thousand pesos of gold: and the rest of the riches that the ship was laden with, was in silks, satins, damasks, with musk and divers other merchandise, and great store of all manner of victuals, with the choice of many conserves of all sorts for to eat, and of sundry sorts of very good wines. These things being made known to the General by the aforesaid captain and pilot, they were commanded to stay aboard the *Desire*, and on the 6 day of November following we went into a harbour which is called by the Spaniards Aguada Segura, or Puerto Seguro.

Here the whole company of the Spaniards, both of

men and women to the number of 190 persons, were set
on shore: where they had a fair river of fresh water,
with great store of fresh fish, fowl, and wood, and also
many hares and coneys upon the main land. Our
General also gave them great store of victuals, of
garbanzos, peason, and some wine. Also they had all
the sails of their ship to make them tents on shore,
with licence to take such store of planks as should be
sufficient to make them a bark. Then we fell to
hoising in of our goods, sharing of the treasure, and
allotting to every man his portion. In division whereof, the eight of this month, many of the company fell
into a mutiny against our General, especially those
which were in the *Content*, which nevertheless were
after a sort pacified for the time.

On the 17 day of November, which is the day of the
happy Coronation of her Majesty, our General commanded all his ordnance to be shot off, with the small
shot both in his own ship where himself went, and
also in the *Content*, which was our Vice-admiral. This
being done, the same night we had many fireworks and
more ordnance discharged, to the great admiration of
all the Spaniards which were there: for the most part
of them had never seen the like before.

This ended, our General discharged the captain,
gave him a royal reward, with provision for his defence
against the Indians, and his company, both of swords,
targets, pieces, shot, and powder, to his great contentment: but before his departure, he took out of this
great ship two young lads born in Japan, which could
both write and read their own language. The eldest,
being about 20 years old, was named Christopher, the
other was called Cosmus, about 17 years of age, both

of very good capacity. He took also with him out of their ship, 3 boys born in the isles of Manilla, the one about 15, the other about 13, and the youngest about 9 years old. The name of the eldest was Alphonso, the second Anthony de Dasi, the third remaineth with the Right Honourable the Countess of Essex. He also took from them one Nicholas Roderigo, a Portugal, who hath not only been in Canton and other parts of China, but also in the islands of Japan, being a country most rich in silver mines, and hath also been in the Philippinas.

He took also from them a Spaniard whose name was Thomas de Ersola, which was a very good pilot from Acapulco and the coast of Nueva España unto the islands of Ladrones, where the Spaniards do put in to water, sailing between Acapulco and the Philippinas. In which isles of Ladrones, they find fresh water, plantains, and potato roots: howbeit the people be very rude and heathens. The 19 day of November aforesaid, about 3 of the clock in the afternoon, our General caused the king's ship to be set on fire, which, having to the quantity of 500 tons of goods in her, we saw burnt unto the water, and then gave them a piece of ordnance and set sail joyfully homewards towards England with a fair wind, which by this time was come about to east-north-east. And night growing near, we left the *Content* astern of us, which was not as yet come out of the road. And here, thinking she would have overtaken us, we lost her company and never saw her after. We were sailing from this haven of Aguada Segura, in California, unto the isles of Ladrones the rest of November, and all December, and so forth until the 3 of January 1588, with a fair wind for the space of 45 days: and we esteemed it to be between 17 and 18 hundred leagues. The 3 day of

January by six of the clock in the morning we had
sight of one of the islands of Ladrones called the island
of Guana, standing in 13⅔ degrees toward the north,
and sailing with a gentle gale before the wind, by 1 or 2
of the clock in the afternoon, we were come up within
2 leagues of the island, where we met with 60 or 70 sails
of canoas full of savages, who came off to sea unto us,

Boat of Savages

and brought with them in their boats plantains, cocos,
potato roots, and fresh fish, which they had caught at
sea, and held them up unto us for to truck or exchange
with us; which when we perceived, we made fast little
pieces of old iron upon small cords and fishing-lines, and
so veered the iron unto their canoas, and they caught
hold of them and took off the iron, and in exchange of
it they would make fast unto the same line either a
potato root, or a bundle of plantains, which we haled

in: and thus our company exchanged with them until they had satisfied themselves with as much as did content them: yet we could not be rid of them. For afterward they were so thick about the ship, that it stemmed and brake 1 or 2 of their canoas; but the men saved themselves, being in every canoa 4, 6, or 8 persons, all naked, and excellent swimmers and divers. They are of a tawny colour and marvellous fat, and bigger ordinarily of stature than the most part of our men in England, wearing their hair marvellous long; yet some of them have it made up and tied with a knot on the crown, and some with 2 knots, much like unto their images which we saw them have, carved in wood, and standing in the head of their boats like unto the images of the devil. Their canoas were as artificially made as any that ever we had seen, considering they were made and contrived without any edge-tool. They are not above half a yard in breadth, and in length some seven or eight yards, and their heads and sterns are both alike; they are made out with rafts of canes and reeds on the starboard side, with mast and sail: their sail is made of mats of sedges, square or triangle-wise, and they sail as well right against the wind, as before the wind. These savages followed us so long, that we could not be rid of them, until in the end our General commanded some half dozen arquebuses to be made ready; and himself struck one of them and the rest shot at them: but they were so yare and nimble, that we could not discern whether they were killed or no, because they could fall backward into the sea and prevent us by diving.

The 14 day of January lying at hull with our ship all the middle watch, from 12 at night until four in the

morning, by the break of day we fell with a headland
of the isles of the Philippinas, which is called Cabo del
Spirito Santo, which is of very great bigness and length,
high land in the midst of it, and very low land as the
cape lieth east and west, trending far into the sea to
the westward. This cape or island is distant from the
isle of Guana, one of the Ladrones, 310 leagues. We
were in sailing of this course eleven days, with scant
winds and some foul weather, bearing no sail two or
three nights. This island standeth in 13 degrees, and
is a place much peopled with heathen people, and all
woody through the whole land: and it is short of the
chiefest island of the Philippinas, called Manilla, about
60 leagues. Manilla is well planted and inhabited with
Spaniards to the number of six or seven hundred
persons: which dwell in a town unwalled, which hath
3 or 4 small block-houses, part made of wood, and part
of stone, being indeed of no great strength: they have
one or two small galleys belong to the town. It is
a very rich place of gold and many other commodities;
and they have yearly traffic from Acapulco in Nueva
España, and also 20 or 30 ships from China and from
the Sanguelos, which bring them many sorts of merchandise. The merchants of China and the Sanguelos
are part Moors and part heathen people. They bring
great store of gold with them, which they traffic and
exchange for silver, and give weight for weight. These
Sanguelos are men of marvellous capacity in devising
and making all manner of things, especially in all handi-
crafts and sciences: and every one is so expert, perfect,
and skilful in his faculty, as few or no Christians are
able to go beyond them in that which they take in
hand. For drawing and embroidering upon satin, silk,

or lawn, either beast, fowl, fish, or worm, for liveliness and perfectness, both in silk, silver, gold, and pearl, they excel. Also the 14 day at night we entered the straits between the island of Luzon, and the island of Camlaia.

The fifteenth of January we fell with an island called Capul, and had betwixt the said island and another island but a narrow passage, and a marvellous rippling of a very great tide with a ledge of rocks lying off the point of the island of Capul : and no danger, but water enough a fair breadth off, and within the point a fair bay and a very good harbour in four fathoms water hard aboard the shore within a cable's length. About 10 of the clock in the morning we came to an anchor.

Our ship was no sooner come to an anchor, but presently there came a canoa rowing aboard us, where-in was one of the chief caciques of the island, whereof there be seven, who supposing that we were Spaniards, brought us potato roots, which they call camotas, and green cocos, in exchange whereof we gave his company pieces of linen, to the quantity of a yard for four cocos, and as much linen for a basket of potato roots of a quart in quantity ; which roots are very good meat, and excellent sweet either roasted or boiled.

This cacique's skin was carved and cut with sundry and many streaks and devices all over his body. We kept him still aboard, and caused him to send those men which brought him aboard back to the island to cause the rest of the principals to come aboard : who were no sooner gone on shore, but presently the people of the island came down with their cocos and potato roots, and the rest of the principals likewise came aboard and brought with them hens and hogs : and they used the same order with us which they do with the Spaniards. For they took for every hog (which they call balboye) eight reals of plate, and for every hen or cock one real of plate. Thus we rode at anchor all that day, doing nothing but buying roots, cocos, hens, hogs, and such things as they brought, refreshing ourselves marvellously well.

The same day at night, being the fifteenth of January 1588, Nicolas Roderigo the Portugal, whom we took out of the great *Santa Anna*, at the Cape of California, desired to speak with our General in secret : which when our General understood, he sent for him, and asked him what he had to say unto him. The Portugal made him this answer, that although he had offended his worship heretofore, yet now he had vowed his faith and true service unto him, and in respect thereof he neither could nor would conceal such treason as was in working against him and his company, and that was this :—that the Spaniard which was taken out of the great *Santa Anna* for a pilot, whose name was Thomas de Ersola, had written a letter, and secretly sealed it and locked it up in his chest, meaning to convey it by the inhabitants of this island to Manilla, the contents whereof were : That there had been two English ships along the coast of Chili, Peru, Nueva España, and Nueva Galicia, and that they had taken many ships and merchandise in them, and burnt divers towns, and spoiled all that ever they could come unto, and that they had taken the king's ship which came from Manilla and all his treasure, with all the merchandise that was therein ; and had set all the people on shore, taking himself away perforce. Therefore he willed them that they should make strong their bulwarks with their two galleys, and all such provision as they could possibly make. He further signified, that we were riding at an island called Capul, which was at the end of the island of Manilla, being but one ship with small force in it, and that the other ship, as he supposed, was gone for the North-west Passage, standing in 55 degrees: and that if they could use any means to surprise us being there at an anchor, they should dispatch it: for our force was but small, and our men but weak, and that the place where we rode was but 50 leagues from them. Otherwise if they let us escape, within few years they must make account to have their town besieged and sacked with an army of English. This information being given, our General called for him, and charged him with these things, which at the first he utterly denied: but in the end, the matter being made manifest and known of certainty by especial trial and proofs, the next morning our General willed that he should be hanged: which was accordingly performed the 16 of January.

We rode for the space of nine days about this island of Capul, where we had divers kinds of fresh victuals, with excellent fresh water in every bay, and great store of wood. The people of this island go almost all naked, and are tawny of colour. The men wear only a strap about their waists, of some kind of linen of their own weaving, which is made of plantain leaves.

These people wholly worship the devil, and often times have conference with him, which appeareth unto them in most ugly and monstrous shape.

On the 23 day of January, our General, Master Thomas Cavendish, caused all the principals of this island, and of a hundred islands more, which he had made to pay tribute unto him (which tribute was in hogs,

hens, potatoes, and cocos), to appear before him, and
made himself and his company known unto them, that
they were Englishmen, and enemies to the Spaniards:
and thereupon spread his ensign and sounded up the
drums, which they much marvelled at: to conclude,
they promised both themselves and all the islands thereabout to aid him, whensoever he should come again
to overcome the Spaniards. Also our General gave
them, in token that we were enemies to the Spaniards,
money back again for all their tribute which they had
paid; which they took marvellous friendly, and rowed
about our ship to show us pleasure marvellous swiftly:
at the last our General caused a saker to be shot off,
whereat they wondered, and with great contentment
took their leaves of us.

The next day being the twenty four of January, we
set sail about six of the clock in the morning, and ran
along the coast of the island of Manilla, shaping our
course north-west between the isle of Manilla, and the
isle of Masbat.

The 28 day in the morning about 7 of the clock,
riding at an anchor betwixt 2 islands, we spied a frigate
under her two courses, coming out between 2 other
islands, which as we imagined came from Manilla, sailing
close aboard the shore along the main island of Panama:
we chased this frigate along the shore, and got very fast
upon it, until in the end we came so near that it stood
into the shore close by a wind, until she was becalmed
and was driven to strike her sail, and banked up with
her oars; whereupon we came unto an anchor with our
ship, a league and a half from the place where the
frigate rowed in; and manned our boat with half a
dozen shot and as many men with swords, which did

row the boat: thus we made after the frigate which had hoised sail and ran into a river, which we could not find. But as we rowed along the shore, our boat came into very shallow water, where many weirs and sticks were set up in divers places in the sea, from whence 2 or 3 canoas came forth, whereof one made somewhat near unto us, with 3 or 4 Indians in it. We called unto them, but they would not come nearer unto us, but rowed from us: whom we durst not follow too far from fear of bringing ourselves too much to the leeward of our ship. Here, as we looked about us, we espied another balsa or canoa of a great bigness, which they which were in her did set along, as we do usually set a barge, with long staves or poles, which was builded up with great canes, and below hard by the water made to row with oars; wherein were about 5 or 6 Indians and one Spaniard. Now as we were come almost at the balsa, we ran aground with our boat; but one or two of our men leaped overboard and freed it again presently, and keeping thwart her head, we laid her aboard and took into us the Spaniard, but the Indians leaped into the sea and dived and rose far off again from us. Presently upon the taking of this canoa, there showed upon the sand a band of soldiers marching with an ensign having a red cross like the flag of England, which were about 50 or 60 Spaniards, which were lately come from Manilla to that town which is called Ragaun in a bark to fetch a new ship of the king's, which was building in a river within the bay, and stayed there but for certain irons that did serve for the rudder of the said ship, which they looked for every day.

This band of men shot at us from the shore with their muskets, but hit none of us, and we shot at them

again : they also manned a frigate and sent it out after
our boat to have taken us. But we with sail and oars
went from them ; and when they perceived that they
could not fetch us, but that they must come within
danger of the ordnance of our ship, they stood in with
the shore again and landed their men, and presently
sent their frigate about the point, but whither we knew
not. So we came aboard with this one Spaniard, which
was neither soldier nor sailor, but one that was come
among the rest from Manilla, and had been in the
hospital there a long time before, and was a very simple
soul, and such a one as could answer to very little that
he was asked, concerning the state of the country. Here
we rode at anchor all that night, and perceived that the
Spaniards had dispersed their band into 2 or 3 parts,
and kept great watch in several steads with fires and
shooting off their pieces. This island hath much plain
ground in it in many places, and many fair and straight
trees do grow upon it, fit for to make excellent good
masts for all sorts of ships. There are also mines of very
fine gold in it, which are in the custody of the Indians.
And to the southward of this place, there is another
very great island, which is not subdued by the Spaniards,
nor any other nation. The people which inhabit it are
all negroes ; and the island is called the Island of Negroes,
and is almost as big as England, standing in 9 degrees :
the most part of it seemeth to be very low land, and by
all likelihood is very fruitful.

The 29 day of January about six of the clock in the
morning we set sail, sending our boat before until it
was two of the clock in the afternoon, passing all this
time as it were through a strait betwixt the said 2
islands of Panama, and the Island of Negroes, and about

16 leagues off we espied a fair opening, trending south-west and by south, at which time our boat came aboard, and our General sent commendations to the Spanish captain, which we came from the evening before, by the Spaniard which we took, and willed him to provide good store of gold; for he meant for to see him with his company at Manilla within few years, and that he did but want a bigger boat to have landed his men, or else he would have seen him then; and so caused him to be set on shore.

The 8 day of February by 8 of the clock in the morning we espied an island near Gilolo, called Batochina, which standeth in one degree from the equinoctial line northward.

The 14 day of February we fell with 11 or 12 very small islands, lying very low and flat, full of trees, and passed by some islands which be sunk and have the dry sands lying in the main sea. These islands, near the Malucos, stand in 3 degrees and 10 minutes to the southward of the line.

On the 17 day, one John Gameford, a cooper, died, which had been sick of an old disease a long time. The 20 day we fell with certain other islands which had many small islands among them, standing 4 degrees to the southward of the line. On the 21 day of February, being Ash Wednesday, Captain Havers died of a most fervent and pestilent ague, which held him furiously some 7 or 8 days, to the no small grief of our General and of all the rest of the company, who caused two falcons and one saker to be shot off, with all the small shot in the ship; who, after he was shrouded in a sheet and a prayer said, was heaved overboard with great lamentation of us all. Moreover, presently after his death myself with divers others in the ship fell marvellously sick, and so continued in very great pain for the space of three weeks or a month by reason of the extreme heat and intemperateness of the climate.

The first day of March, having passed through the straits of Java Minor and Java Major, we came to an anchor under the south-west parts of Java Major: where we espied certain of the people which were fishing by the sea-side in a bay which was under the island. Then our General taking into the ship-boat certain of his company, and a negro which could speak the Morisco tongue, which he had taken out of the great *St Anna*, made toward those fishers, which having espied our boat ran on shore into the wood for fear of our men: but our General caused his negro to call unto them; who no sooner heard him call, but presently one of them came out to the shore-side and made answer. Our General by the negro enquired of him for fresh water, which they found, and caused the fisher to go to the king and to certify him of a ship that was come to have traffic for victuals, and for diamonds, pearls, or any other rich jewels that he had: for which he should have either gold or other merchandise in exchange. The fisher answered that we should have all manner of victuals that we would request. Thus the boat came aboard again. Within a while after we went about to furnish our ship throughly with wood and water.

About the eighth of March two or three canoas came from the town unto us with eggs, hens, fresh fish, oranges, and limes, and brought word we should have had victuals more plentifully, but that they were so far to be brought to us where we rid. Which when our General heard he weighed anchor and stood in nearer for the town. And as we were under sail we met with one of the king's canoas coming toward us: whereupon we shook the ship in the wind and stayed for the canoa until it came aboard of us, and stood into the bay which was hard by and came to an anchor. In this canoa was the king's secretary, who had on his head a piece of dyed linen cloth folded up like a Turk's tuliban; he was all naked saving about his waist; his breast was carved with the broad arrow upon it; he went barefooted; he had an interpreter with him, which was a mestizo, that is, half an Indian and half a Portugal, who could speak very good Portuguese. This secretary signified unto our General that he had brought him a hog, hens, eggs, fresh fish, sugar-canes, and wine (which wine was as strong as any aqua vitae, and as clear as any rock water). He told him further that he would bring victuals so sufficiently for him, as he and his company would request, and that within the space of four days. Our General used him singularly well, banqueted him most royally with the choice of many and sundry conserves, wines both sweet and other, and caused his musicians to make him music. This done our General told him that he and his company were Englishmen; and that we had been at China and had had traffic there with them, and that we were come thither to discover, and purposed to go to Malacca. The people of Java told our General that there were certain Portugals in the island which lay there as factors continually to traffic with them, to buy negroes, cloves, pepper, sugar, and many other commodities. This secretary of the king with his interpreter lay one night aboard our ship. The same night, because they lay aboard, in the evening at the setting of the watch, our

General commanded every man in the ship to provide
his arquebus and his shot, and so with shooting off 40
or 50 small shot and one saker, himself set the watch
with them. This was no small marvel unto these
heathen people, who had not commonly seen any ship
so furnished with men and ordnance. The next morning we dismissed the secretary and his interpreter with
all humanity.

The fourth day after, which was the 12 of March,
according to their appointment came the king's canoas;
but the wind being somewhat scant they could not get
aboard that night, but put into a bay under the island
until the next day. And presently after the break of day
there came to the number of 9 or 10 of the king's canoas
so deeply laden with victuals as they could swim, with
two great live oxen, half a score of wonderful great and
fat hogs, a number of hens which were alive, drakes,
geese, eggs, plantains, sugar-canes, sugar in plates,
cocos, sweet oranges and sour, limes, great store of
wine and aqua vitae, salt to season victuals withal, and
almost all manner of victuals else, with divers of the
king's officers which were there. Among all the rest of
the people in one of these canoas came two Portugals,
which were of middle stature, and men of marvellous
proper personage; they were each of them in a loose
jerkin, and hose, which came down from the waist to
the ankle, because of the use of the country, and partly
because it was Lent, and a time for doing of their
penance (for they account it as a thing of great dislike
among these heathens to wear either hose or shoes on
their feet): they had on each of them a very fair and
a white lawn shirt, with falling bands on the same,
very decently, only their bare legs excepted. These

Portugals were no small joy unto our General and all the rest of our company; for we had not seen any Christian, that was our friend, of a year and a half before. Our General used and treated them singularly well, with banquets and music. They told us that they were no less glad to see us, than we to see them, and enquired of the estate of their country, and what was become of Don Antonio, their king, and whether he were living or no; for that they had not of long time been in Portugal, and that the Spaniards had always brought them word that he was dead. Then our General satisfied them in every demand; assuring them that their king was alive, and in England, and had honourable allowance of our queen, and that there was war between Spain and England, and that we were come under the King of Portugal into the South Sea, and had warred upon the Spaniards there, and had fired, spoiled, and sunk all the ships along that coast that we could meet withal, to the number of eighteen or twenty sails. With this report they were sufficiently satisfied.

On the other side they declared unto us the state of the island of Java. First the plentifulness and great choice and store of victuals of all sorts, and of all manner of fruits, as before is set down. Then the great and rich merchandise which are there to be had. Then they described the properties and nature of the people as followeth. The name of the king of that part of the island was Rajah Bolamboam, who was a man had in great majesty and fear among them. The common people may not bargain, sell, or exchange anything with any other nation without special licence from their king: and if any so do, it is present death for him. The king himself is a man of great years, and hath a hundred wives; his son hath fifty. The custom of the country is, that whensoever the king doth die, they take the body so dead and burn it and preserve the ashes of him, and within five days next after, the wives of the said king so dead, according to the custom and use of their country, every one of them go together to a place appointed, and the chief of the women, which was nearest unto him in account, hath a ball in her hand and throweth it from her, and to the place where the ball resteth, thither they go all, and turn their faces to the eastward, and every one with a dagger in their hand, (which dagger they call a crise, and is as sharp as a razor) stab themselves to the heart, and with their hands all-to bebathe themselves in their own blood, and falling grovelling on their faces so end their days. This thing is as true as it seemeth to any hearer to be strange.

The men of themselves be very politic and subtle, and singularly valiant, being naked men, in any action they undertake, and wonderfully at commandment and fear of their king. For example: if their king command them to undertake any exploit, be it never so dangerous or desperate, they dare not nor will not refuse it, though they die every man in the execution of the same. For he will cut off the heads of every one of them which return alive without bringing of their purpose to pass: which is such a thing among them, as it maketh them the most valiant people in all the south-east parts of the world; for they never fear any death. For being in fight with any nation, if any of them feeleth himself hurt with lance or sword, he will willingly run himself upon the weapon quite through his body to procure his death the more speedily, and in this desperate sort end his days, or overcome his enemy. Moreover, although the men be tawny of colour and go continually naked, yet their women be fair of complexion and go more apparelled.

After they had thus described the state of the island, and the orders and fashions of the people, they told us farther, that if their king Don Antonio would come unto them, they would warrant him to have all the Malucos at commandment, besides China, Sangles, and the isles of the Philippinas, and that he might be assured to have all the Indians on his side that are in the country. After we had fully contented these Portugals, and the people of Java which brought us victuals in their canoas, they took their leave of us with promise of all good entertainment at our returns, and our General gave them three great pieces of ordnance at their departing. Thus the next day, being the 16 of March, we set sail towards the Cape of Good Hope, called by the Portugals Cabo de Buena Esperanza, on the southermost coast of Africa.

The rest of March and all the month of April we spent in traversing that mighty and vast sea, between the isle of Java and the main of Africa, observing the heavens, the Crosiers or South-pole, the other stars, the fowls, which are marks unto the seamen of fair weather, foul weather, approaching of lands or islands, the winds, the tempests, the rains and thunders, with the alterations of tides and currents.

The 10 day of May we had a storm at the west, and it blew so hard that it was as much as the ship could stir close by under the wind; and the storm continued all that day and all that night.

The next day, being the 11 of May, in the morning, one of the company went into the top, and espied land bearing north, and north and by west of us, and about noon we espied land to bear west of us, which as we did imagine was the Cape of Buena Esperanza, whereof indeed we were short some 40 or 50 leagues. And by reason of the scantness of the wind we stood along to the south-east until midnight; at which time the wind came fair, and we haled along westward.

The 12 and 13 days we were becalmed, and the sky was very hazy and thick until the 14 day at three of the clock in the afternoon, at which time the sky cleared, and we espied the land again which was the cape called Cabo Falso, which is short of the Cape de Buena Esperanza 40 or 50 leagues. This Cape is very easy to be known. For there are right over it three very high hills standing but a small way one off another, and the highest standeth in the midst, and the ground is much lower by the seaside. The Cape of Good Hope beareth west and by south from the said Cabo Falso.

The 16 day of May, about 4 of the clock in the afternoon, the wind came up at east a very stiff gale, which held until it was Saturday with as much wind as ever the ship could go before: at which time, by six of the clock in the morning, we espied the promontory or headland, called the Cape de Buena Esperanza, which is a reasonable high land, and at the westermost point a little off the main do show two hummocks, the one upon the other, and three other hummocks lying further off into the sea, yet low land between and adjoining unto the sea.

This Cape of Buena Esperanza is set down and accounted for two thousand leagues from the island of Java in the Portugal sea-charts; but it is not so much almost by an hundred and fifty leagues, as we found by the running of our ship. We were in running of these eighteen hundred and fifty leagues just nine weeks.

The eighth day of June by break of day we fell in sight of the island of St Helena, seven or eight leagues short of it, having but a small gale of wind, or almost none at all: insomuch as we could not get into it that day, but stood off and on all that night.

The next day, being the 9 of June, having a pretty easy gale of wind, we stood in with the shore, our boat being sent away before to make the harbour; and about one of the clock in the afternoon we came unto an anchor in 12 fathoms water two or three cables' length from the shore, in a very fair and smooth bay under the north-west side of the island.

This island is very high land, and lieth in the main sea, standing as it were in the midst of the sea between the mainland of Africa and the main of Brasilia and the coast of Guinea, and is in 15 degrees and 48 minutes to the southward of the equinoctial line, and is distant from the Cape of Buena Esperanza between 5 and 6 hundred leagues.

The same day about two or three of the clock in the afternoon we went on shore, where we found a marvellous fair and pleasant valley, wherein divers handsome buildings and houses were set up, and especially one which was a church, which was tiled and whited on the outside very fair, and made with a porch, and within the church at the upper end was set an altar, whereon stood a very large table set in a frame having in it the picture of our Saviour Christ upon the cross and the image of our Lady praying, with divers other histories curiously painted in the same. The sides of the church were all hanged with stained cloths having many devices drawn in them.

There are two houses adjoining to the church, on each side one, which serve for kitchens to dress meat in, with necessary rooms and houses of office. The coverings of the said houses are made flat, whereon is planted a very fair vine, and through both the said houses runneth a very good and wholesome stream of fresh water.

There is also, right over against the said church, a fair causey made up with stones reaching unto a valley by the seaside, in which valley is planted a garden, wherein grow great store of pompions and melons. And upon the said causey is a frame erected whereon hang two bells wherewith they ring to mass; and hard unto it is a cross set up, which is squared, framed, and made very artificially of freestone, whereon is carved in cyphers what time it was builded, which was in the year of our Lord 1571.

This valley is the fairest and largest low plot in all the island, and it is marvellous sweet and pleasant, and planted in every place either with fruit trees, or with herbs. There are fig trees, which bear fruit continually, and marvellous plentifully; for on every tree you shall have blossoms, green figs, and ripe figs, all at once; and it is so all the year long. The reason is that the island standeth so near the sun. There be also great store of lemon trees, orange trees, pomegranate trees, pome-citron trees, date trees, which bear fruit as the fig trees do, and are planted carefully and very artificially with very pleasant walks under and between them, and the said walks be overshadowed with the leaves of the trees. And in every void place is planted parsley, sorrel, basil, fennel, aniseed, mustard seed, radishes, and many special good herbs: and the fresh water brook runneth through divers places of this orchard, and may with very small pains be made to water any one tree in the valley.

This fresh water stream cometh from the tops of the mountains, and falleth from the cliff into the valley the height of a cable, and hath many arms out of it, which refresh the whole island, and almost every tree in it. The island is altogether high mountains and steep valleys, except it be in the tops of some hills, and down below in some of the valleys, where marvellous store of all these kinds of fruits before spoken of do grow. There is greater store growing in the tops of the mountains than below in the valleys: but it is wonderful laboursome and also dangerous travelling up unto them and down again, by reason of the height and steepness of the hills.

There is also upon this island great store of partridges, which are very tame, not making any great haste to fly away though one come very near them, but only to run away, and get up into the steep cliffs: we killed some of them with a fowling-piece. They differ very much from our partridges which are in England both in bigness and also in colour. For they be within a little as big as a hen, and are of an ash colour, and live in coveys twelve, sixteen, and twenty together: you cannot go ten or twelve score but you shall see or spring one or two coveys at the least.

There are likewise no less store of pheasants in the island, which are also marvellous big and fat, surpassing those which are in our country in bigness and in numbers of a company. They differ not very much in colour from the partridges before spoken of.

We found moreover in this place great store of
Guinea cocks, which we call turkeys, of colour black
and white, with red heads: they are much about the
same bigness which ours be of in England. Their eggs
be white, and as big as a turkey's egg.

There are in this island thousands of goats, which the
Spaniards call cabritos, which are very wild: you shall
see one or two hundred of them together, and sometimes
you may behold them going in a flock almost a mile
long. Some of them (whether it be the nature of the
breed of them, or of the country I wot not) are as big as
an ass, with a mane like a horse and a beard hanging
down to the very ground. They will climb up the cliffs,
which are so steep that a man would think it a thing
impossible for any living thing to go there. We took
and killed many of them for all their swiftness; for
there be thousands of them upon the mountains.

Here are in like manner great store of swine, which
be very wild and very fat, and of a marvellous bigness.
They keep altogether upon the mountains, and will very
seldom abide any man to come near them, except it be
by mere chance when they be found asleep, or otherwise, according to their kind, be taken laid in the mire.

We found in the houses at our coming 3 slaves
which were negroes, and one which was born in the
island of Java, which told us that the East Indian
fleet, which were in number 5 sails, the least whereof
were in burthen 8 or 900 tons, all laden with spices and
Calicut cloth, with store of treasure and very rich stones
and pearls, were gone from the said island of St Helena
but 20 days before we came thither.

This island hath been found of long time by the
Portugals, and hath been altogether planted by them,

for their refreshing as they come from the East Indies. And when they come they have all things plentiful for their relief, by reason that they suffer none to inhabit there that might spend up the fruit of the island, except some very few sick persons in their company, which they stand in doubt will not live until they come home, whom they leave there to refresh themselves, and take away the year following in the other fleet if they live so long. They touch here rather in their coming home from the East Indies, than at their going thither, because they are throughly furnished with corn when they set out of Portugal, but are but meanly victualled at their coming from the Indies, where there groweth little corn.

The 20 day of June, having taken in wood and water, and refreshed ourselves with such things as we found there, and made clean our ship, we set sail about 8 of the clock in the night toward England. At our setting sail we had the wind at south-east, and we haled away north-west and by west. The wind is commonly off the shore at this island of St Helena.

On Wednesday, being the third day of July, we went away north-west, the wind being still at south-east; at which time we were in 1 degree and 48 minutes to the southward of the equinoctial line.

The twelfth day of the said month of July it was very little wind, and toward night it was calm and blew no wind at all, and so continued until it was Monday, being the 15 day of July.

On Wednesday, the 17 day of the abovesaid month, we had the wind scant at west-north-west. We found the wind continually to blow at east, and north-east, and east-north-east after we were in 3 or 4 degrees to the northward; and it altered not until we came between 30 and 40 degrees to the northward of the equinoctial line.

On Wednesday, the 21 day of August, the wind came up at south-west a fair gale: by which day at noon we were in 38 degrees of northerly latitude.

On Friday, in the morning, being the 23 day of August, at four of the clock we haled east, and east and by south for the northermost islands of the Azores.

On Saturday, the 24 day of the said month, by 5 of the clock in the morning, we fell in sight of the two islands of Flores and Corvo, standing in 39 degrees and ½, and sailed away north-east.

The third of September we met with a Flemish hulk which came from Lisbon, and declared unto us the overthrowing of the Spanish Fleet, to the singular rejoicing and comfort of us all.

The 9 of September, after a terrible tempest which carried away most part of our sails, by the merciful favour of the Almighty we recovered our long-wished port of Plymouth in England, from whence we set forth at the beginning of our voyage.

A LETTER OF MASTER THOMAS CAVENDISH TO THE RIGHT HONOURABLE THE LORD HUNSDON, LORD CHAMBERLAIN, ONE OF HER MAJESTY'S MOST HONOURABLE PRIVY COUNCIL, TOUCHING THE SUCCESS OF HIS VOYAGE ABOUT THE WORLD.

Right Honourable, as your favour heretofore hath been most greatly extended towards me, so I humbly desire a continuance thereof: and though there be no means in me to deserve the same, yet the uttermost of my services shall not be wanting, whensoever it shall please your honour to dispose thereof. I am humbly to desire your honour to make known unto her Majesty the desire I have had to do her Majesty service in the performance of this voyage. And as it hath pleased God to give her the victory over part of her enemies, so I trust ere long to see her overthrow them all. For the places of their wealth, whereby they have maintained and made their wars, are now perfectly discovered; and if it please her Majesty, with a very small power she may take the spoil of them all. It hath pleased the Almighty to suffer me to circumpass the whole globe of the world, entering in at the Strait of Magellan, and returning by the Cape de Buena Esperanza. In which voyage, I have either discovered or brought certain intelligence of all the rich places of the world, that ever were known or discovered by any Christian. I navigated alongst the coast of Chili, Peru, and Nueva España, where I made great spoils: I burnt and sunk 19 sails of ships small and great. All the villages and towns that ever I landed at, I burnt and spoiled: and had I not been discovered upon the coast, I had taken great quantity of treasure. The matter of most profit unto me was a great ship of the king's which I took at California, which ship came from the Philippinas, being one of the richest of merchandise that ever passed those seas, as the king's register and merchants' accounts did show; for it did amount in value to [1] in Mexico to be sold. Which goods (for that my ships were not able to contain the least part of them) I was enforced to set on fire. From the Cape of California, being the

---

[1] Blank in the original.

uttermost part of all Nueva España, I navigated to the Islands of the Philippinas hard upon the coast of China; of which country I have brought such intelligence as hath not been heard of in these parts. The stateliness and riches of which country I fear to make report of, lest I should not be credited: for if I had not known sufficiently the incomparable wealth of that country, I should have been as incredulous thereof, as others will be that have not had the like experience. I sailed along the Islands of the Malucos, where among some of the heathen people I was well entreated, where our countrymen may have trade as freely as the Portugals, if they will themselves. From thence I passed by the Cape of Buena Esperanza, and found out by the way homeward the island of St Helena, where the Portugals use to relieve themselves; and from that island God hath suffered me to return into England. All which services with myself I humbly prostrate at her Majesty's feet, desiring the Almighty long to continue her reign among us: for at this day she is the most famous and victorious prince that liveth in the world.

Thus humbly desiring pardon of your honour for my tediousness, I leave your lordship to the tuition of the Almighty. Plymouth, this ninth of September 1588.

Your honour's most humble to command,

THOMAS CAVENDISH.

JACOB LE MAIRE AND WILLIAM SCHOUTEN

The Discovery of a New Passage into the Pacific by Cape Horn (1616)

From "The Relation of a Wonderful Voyage made by William Cornelison Schouten of Hoorn, showing how South from the Straits of Magellan, in Terra Del-fuogo, he found and discovered a new passage through the great South Sea, and that way sailed round about the world."

Jacob Le Maire

[Two ships of Hoorn, the *Eendracht* (*Unity*) of 360 tons—William Schouten, master and chief pilot, and Jacob Le Maire, merchant and principal factor—and the *Hoorn* of 110 tons—John Schouten, master—had sailed from Holland on June 14, 1615 to search for a passage into the Pacific south of the Strait of Magellan. By December they had reached Port Desire, and here the *Hoorn* was accidentally burnt, while they were cleaning it by burning reeds underneath.

The *Unity* left this place in the middle of January, and on the 24th they had reached the entrance of Le Maire Strait, and caught sight of Staten Island.]

The 24 [January, 1616] in the morning we saw land on starboard not above a great league distant from us. There we had ground at 40 fathom, and a west wind. The land stretched east and south, with very high hills that were all covered over with ice. We sailed along by that land, and about noon passed it and saw other land east from it, which also was very high and ragged.

These lands, as we guessed, lay about 8 leagues one from the other, and seemed as if there were a good passage between them, which we were the better persuaded unto, for that there ran a hard stream southward between both these lands.

Then about noon we were under 54 degrees 46 minutes, and after noon we had a north wind and made towards this opening, but about evening it calmed and that night we drave forwards with a hard stream, and little wind. There we saw an innumerable number of penguins and thousands of whales, so that we were forced to look well about us, and to wind and turn to shun the whales, lest we should sail upon them.

The 25 in the morning we were close by the east

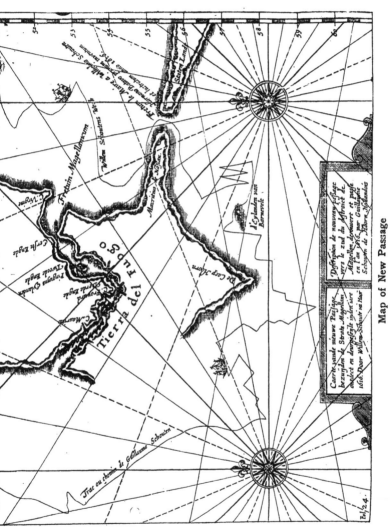

Map of New Passage

land, which was very high and craggy, which on the
north side reacheth east-south-east, as far as we could
see. That land we called States Land, but the land
that lay west from us, we named Maurice Land. We
perceived that on both sides thereof there were good
roads, and sandy bays, for on either side it had sandy
strands and very fair sandy ground. There are great
store of fish, penguins, and porpoises, as also birds, and
water enough, but we could see no trees. We had a
north wind in the entry and went south-south-west
with a stiff course. At noon we were under 55 degrees
36 minutes, and then held our course south-west, with
a good sharp wind and rain, and a stiff gale. We saw
the land on the south side of the passage, upon the
west end of Maurice van Nassau's Land, reach west-
south-west and south-west, as far as we could see it,
all very high and craggy land. In the evening the wind
was south-west, and that night we went south with
great waves or billows out of the south-west, and very
blue water, whereby we judged and held for certain
that we had great deep water to loefward from us,
nothing doubting but that it was the great South Sea.
Whereat we were exceeding glad to think that we had
discovered a way, which until that time was unknown
to men, as afterward we found it to be true.

There we saw extreme great sea-mews, bigger of
body than swans. Their wings being spread abroad
were each of them about a fathom long. These birds,
being unaccustomed to see men, came to our ship, and
sat thereon, and let our men take and kill them.

The 26 we were under 57 degrees, with a flying
storm out of the west and south-west, the whole
quarter, with very high and blue water, we held our

course southward, and in the north-west saw very high land. In the night we turned north-westward.

The 27 we were under 56 degrees 51 minutes, the weather very cold, with hail and rain, the wind west and west by south, and we went southward and then crossed northward with our mainsails.

The 28 we hoised our topsails. Then we had great billows out of the west, with a west wind and then a north-east, and therewith held our course south, and then west and west by south, and were under fifty-six degrees and forty-eight minutes.

The 29 we had a north-east wind, and held our course south-west and saw two islands before us, lying west-south-west from us. About noon we got to them, but could not sail above them, so that we held our course north. About them they had dry gray cliffs, and some low cliffs about them. They lay under 57 degrees southward of the equinoctial line. We named them Barnevelt's Islands. From them we sailed west-north-west. About evening we saw land again, lying north-west and north-north-west from us, which was the land that lay south from the Straits of Magellan, which reacheth southward, all high hilly land covered over with snow, ending with a sharp point, which we called Cape Horn. It lieth under 57 degrees and 48 minutes. Then we had fair weather, and a north wind, with great billows out of the west. We held on course west, and found a strong stream that ran westward.

The 30 we still had great billows out of the west, with hollow water and a strong stream that went westward, which assured us that we had an open way into the South Sea. Then we were under 57 degrees 34 minutes.

Cape Horn

The 31 we had a north wind, and sailed west, and were under 58 degrees. Then the wind turning west, and west-south-west, somewhat variable, we passed by Cape Van Horn, and could see no more land, and had great billows out of the west, and very blue water, which then fully assured us that we had the broad South Sea before us, and no land.......

The 12 [February] our men had each of them three cups of wine in sign of joy for our good hap, for then the Straits of Magellan lay east from us. The same day by advice of all our council, at the request of our chief merchant, the new passage (by us discovered between Mauritius Land and the States Land) was named the Straits of Le Maire, although by good right it should rather have been called William Schouten's Strait, after our master's name, by whose wise conduction and skill in sailing, the same was found.

During the time that we passed through that new strait, and sailing southward about that new found land, till we got to the west side of the Straits of Magellan, for the most part we had a very strong stream, hollow water, continual rain, mists, moist and thick weather, with much hail and snow: whereby we endured much trouble, misery, and disease. But in regard that we had so luckily discovered that passage, and hoping that the places which we were yet to discover would likewise fall out well, we were encouraged, not once thinking upon our former hard passage, with assured minds determined to go forward on our voyage.

NOTES

MAGELLAN'S VOYAGE

The black figures refer to pages and the plain figures to lines

1, 2. five ships. The *Trinidad* or *Trinity* (Flagship, 110 tons): the *San Antonio* (120 tons): the *Conception* (90 tons): the *Victoria* (85 tons): the *Santiago* (75 tons).

11. Emperor. Charles V.

16. very illustrious lord. Pigafetta's narrative is dedicated to Philip de Villiers l'Isle-Adam, grand master of the Knights of St John (Knights of Rhodes until 1530, and afterwards Knights of Malta), 1521—1534.

5, 7. St Lucar. A seaport near Cape St Vincent, where they remained for a time to take in further supplies.

24. an ever-running fountain. There is some foundation for this story, "for both in Madeira and the Canaries the laurel and other heavy-foliaged evergreens condense abundant water from the daily mists." Guillemard's *Magellan*.

30. Siroc. South-east.

6, 16. broach to. To veer and turn the side towards the wind and waves.

28. St Anselm. Or St Elmo. A ball of electric light that appears sometimes in thunderstorms about mastheads and yardarms, and was considered by sailors to be a good omen. The name is probably derived from St Erasmus (Italian, *Eremo*), Bishop of Naples—the patron saint particularly of those who navigated the Mediterranean.

7, 14. Verzin. *Verzino* is the Italian for brazil-wood (a hard red wood, yielding a dye), from which, owing to its abundance there, the name Brazil was given to the country.

9, 28. South Sea. Balboa, the first European who saw the Pacific from the west (Sept. 25, 1513), called it the South Sea. The isthmus of Darien turns to the west, and the Pacific would have been seen to the south.

32. seventeen leagues in width. The Rio de la Plata. According to other accounts Magellan left Rio de Janeiro on Dec. 26, and remained at Rio de la Plata until Feb. 2, 1520. Here he explored the mouth of the river, and sent ships to discover whether it was the entrance to a strait leading into the Pacific.

11, 1. Solis. The discoverer of Rio de la Plata (1516).

6. geese and sea-wolves. Penguins and seals.

28. a port. Port St Julian. They arrived there March 31, 1520, according to the Genoese pilot's account.

12, 9. waist. "Their height appears greater than it really is, from their large guanaco mantles, their long flowing hair, and general figure; on an average their height is about six feet, with some men taller and only a few shorter; and the women are also tall; altogether they are certainly the tallest race which we anywhere saw." Darwin's *Journal during the Voyage of H.M.S. Beagle.*

19. neighs. The guanaco, a kind of llama.

22. shoes. Owing to the size and clumsy look these skins gave their feet, Magellan named them Patagonians ("big feet").

15, 4. Setebos. Shakespeare must have got this word from Eden's *Decades of the Newe Worlde* (1555), which contains a narrative of Magellan's voyage, and probably Caliban was suggested by the account of the Patagonian giants.

Caliban twice refers to the god Setebos. See *Tempest* I. ii, and v. i.

23. Cavagio. An error for Carvalho. He sailed as pilot in the *Conception.*

16, 14. Patagoni. See note p. 12, l. 22.

27. plotted treason. For a full account of this plot, which was far more serious than appears from Pigafetta's narrative, see Guillemard's *Magellan.* The mutineers had seized the *Conception*, the *S. Antonio*, and the *Victoria* before the officers of the flagship suspected the plot. The master of the *Santiago* remained true. Magellan first captured the *Victoria*, and afterwards the other two ships. Quesada was executed, and Juan de Cartagena and a priest marooned. Mendoza had already been killed on the *Victoria.* Forty men were condemned to death for treason, but were afterwards pardoned by Magellan.

31. Quesada. Captain of the *Conception.*

17, 8. St James. The *Santiago.*

16. a river of fresh water. They named it the Santa Cruz.

19, 12. Bohemia. Martin Behaim constructed a celebrated globe at Nuremberg in 1492. The continent of America is absent from it, and Magellan therefore cannot have got any indication of his strait from it.

28. **a corner:** The "First Narrows," just beyond Anegada point.

32. **a bay.** St Philip's Bay.

21, 1. **larger than the first two.** The "Second Narrows" and Broad Reach.

13. **two mouths.** The first is the passage east of Dawson Island leading into Useless Bay and Admiralty Sound. The second is the passage between the west side of Dawson Island and Brunswick Peninsula.

32. **off to Spain.** The *San Antonio* reached Seville, May 6, 1521. Gomez was imprisoned when the *Victoria* returned, but afterwards set free, and went on an exploring expedition to the coast of North America.

22, 11. **Sardines.** Possibly Port Gallant in Brunswick Peninsula.

19. **Cape of Desire.** Now Cape Pillar.

25. **Seranno.** Brother of Magellan's friend Francisco Seranno. He had served under Vasco da Gama and Albuquerque, and had already coasted Brazil. Captain of the *Santiago*, and (after the loss of the *Santiago*) of the *Conception*.

23, 14. **islet.** Santa Magdalena in the north of Broad Reach.

17. **Isles.** Probably the port of San Miguel, near Port Gallant, on Brunswick Peninsula.

24, 3. **missiglioni.** Shell-fish.

26, 10. **died.** They were suffering from scurvy.

27, 33. **Ladrone Islands.** On the day they left these islands (March 9) the only Englishman in the fleet, "Master Andrew," of Bristol, died. He was the master-gunner of the flagship.

28, 4. **Zamal.** Now Samar, in the Philippines.

26. **Uraca.** Arrack.

27. **figs.** Bananas.

28. **cocos.** Coco-nuts.

36, 17. **Zuluan and Calagan.** Butuan and Caraga in the north-east of Mindanao.

39, 4. **Ceylon.** Leyte.

25. **Mazzava.** Limasaua.

28. **Zubu.** Zebu.

49, 27. **balangai.** See p. 32, l. 15.

53, 23. **Barbosa.** Magellan had married Barbosa's sister, Beatrice, probably in 1517.

24. **Seranno.** Really a Portuguese, though possibly a naturalized Spaniard. See note p. 22, l. 25.

54, 1. Beatrice. She diěd in March, 1522, their one son Rodrigo (about six months old at the time of Magellan's departure) having died in September, 1521.

55, 26. the other two. In place of the captains (Barbosa and Seranno) killed at Cebu, Carvalho and Espinosa were chosen. One hundred and fifteen men were left.

28. Panilongon. Panglao.

30. a large island. Mindanao.

57, 27. Cagayan. Cagayan Sulu, north-east of Borneo.

28. Burné. Borneo.

58, 4. Chipit. Quipit, in the north-east of Mindanao.

26. another island. Borneo, the largest island in the world.

60, 15. city. Brunei.

64, 5. On leaving this island. Sept. 27, 1521. Here Carvalho was deposed from the chief command, and again became chief pilot. Espinosa was appointed instead, and Sebastian del Cano captain of the *Victoria*.

65, 12. two pilots. This piratical act is a sign of the loss of discipline among the men since Magellan's death.

66, 10. Tadore. Tidore.

68, 10. Tarenate. Ternate..

69, 11. Francisco Seranno. Magellan's closest friend. In 1509 he had fought with Magellan (on a fleet sent by Almeida to Malacca) against the Malays, and was shipwrecked while returning. In 1511 he went as Captain of a ship to the Moluccas to explore and trade, and after many adventures and another shipwreck went to Ternate, and supported the king against the king of Tidore, by whom he was at last poisoned. Magellan had made use of his letters to persuade the Emperor to agree to the expedition.

19. testoon. Half a ducat. Worth about 4s. 6d.

71, 13. bahar. 406 lbs.

76, 9. St Barbara. The patroness of powder ˙magazines.

17. marcello.. A small silver Venetian coin, struck in 1473 by the Doge Nicolo Marcello.

79, ˙6. divine birds. Birds of Paradise.

81, 29. Carvalho. See note p. 15, l. 23. Of these 53 men only four, including Espinosa, years after, reached Spain.

83, 9. Cape Verde Islands. By this time there were only 31 men left.

11. St James's. Santiago, the most southerly and largest of the islands.

84, 5. was detained. Soon after they were set free, and sent to Lisbon in a ship returning from Calicut. The united crew were then received at court by Charles V, who granted del Cano an annual pension, and a coat-of-arms containing two cinnamon sticks, three nutmegs, and twelve cloves. *Supporters*, two Malay kings holding each a spice branch. *Crest*, a globe with motto, "Primus circumdedisti me" ("Thou art the first man that ever sailed about me").

DRAKE'S VOYAGE

85, 1. South Sea. The Pacific Ocean. See note p. 9, l. 28.

5. five ships and barks. The *Pelican*, Admiral, 100 tons. Captain-general Drake: the *Elizabeth*, Vice-Admiral, 80 tons, Captain John Winter: the *Marigold*, 30 tons: the *Swan,* a fly-boat of 50 tons: the *Benedict*, a pinnace of 15 tons. They took "certain pinnaces ready framed, but carried aboard in pieces, to be new set up in smoother water, when occasion served. Neither had he omitted to make provision also for ornament and delight, carrying to this purpose with him expert musicians, rich furniture...and divers shows of all sorts of curious workmanship." Sir Francis Drake (Drake's nephew), *The World Encompassed by Sir Francis Drake*, 1628. Referred to hereafter as F. D.

8. pretended. Intended.

16, 87, 8. Admiral, General. In a fleet, the commander-in-chief was called the *General* (or *Captain-General*), his ship the *Admiral*: the second in command was the *Lieutenant-General*, sailing in the *Vice-Admiral*.

88, 5. Cape Blanco. The White Cape (so called by its Portuguese discoverers from the colour of the sandy shore), about 21° N. Lat. Cape Verde to the south—The Green Cape (from its vegetation).

24. cabritos. Goats.

89, 26. kerning. Corning, granulating.

90, 23. from the danger. Out of the power.

24. pieces. Guns.

91, 6. retaining the pilot. Nuño da Silva, whose log-book and depositions concerning the voyage are still in existence.

31. bonitos. The Bonito (Spanish for 'good') or Tunny, of the mackerel family, was much esteemed by the Spaniards, and so named by them.

92, 14. experiments. Experiences.

94, 9. good bay. Drake named the place Cape Hope.

25. as were absent. i.e. The *Swan* (the fly-boat) and the Portuguese prize, called the *Mary*.

95, 6. **burnt her.** "Our General...determined to diminish the number of his ships, thereby to draw his men into less room, that both the fewer ships might the better keep company, and that they might also be the better appointed with new and fresh supplies of provision and men, one to ease the burthen of another." F. D.

15. **to deliver.** To do any business.

30. **Cape of Good Hope.** See note p. 94, l. 9.

96, 7. **Thomas Drake.** Francis Drake's brother.

11. **in his draught.** In drawing it.

14. **to their shifts.** To use expedients.

97, 22. **St Julian.** Here they abandoned the *Mary* (Portuguese prize), "because she was leak and troublesome," and so "brought our fleet into the smallest number, even three only." F. D.

23. **Freat.** Latin, *fretum*, a strait.

33. **In this Strait.** Here "in remembrance of his honourable friend and favourer, Sir Christopher Hatton, he changed the name of the ship which himself went in from the *Pelican* to be called the *Golden Hind*." F. D. The Golden Hind was Hatton's crest.

98, 30. **fowl which could not fly.** Penguins. "They have no wings, but short pinions which serve their turn in swimming. Their colour is somewhat black mixed with white spots under their belly, and about their neck. They walk so upright, that afar off a man would take them to be little children. If a man approach anything near them, they run into holes in the ground (which be not very deep), whereof the island is full. So that to take them we had staves with hooks fast to the ends, wherewith some of our men pulled them out and others being ready with cudgels did knock them on the head, for they bite so cruelly with their crooked bills, that none of us was able to handle them alive." Edward Cliffe's account of Winter's voyage in the *Elizabeth*.

99, 11. **amend us a whit.** They were no worse off while the eclipse lasted, and no better off when it ceased. This violent storm lasted (according to F. D.) for fifty-two days, and in it the *Marigold* sank with all her crew.

16. **tierce.** A third. Here they may have seen Cape Horn (afterwards discovered, and rounded for the first time, by the Dutch). F. D. says, "The uttermost cape or headland of all these islands stands near in 56 deg., without which there is no main nor island to be seen to the southwards, but that the Atlantic Ocean and the South Sea meet in a most large and free scope. It hath been a dream through many ages that these islands have been a main, and that it hath been *terra incognita*, wherein many strange monsters lived." Drake named one of these islands Elizabeth Island.

28. Master Winter was. The *Elizabeth* sailed back through the Straits—the Spaniards had spread reports that it was impossible to do this owing to the current—and reached England on June 2, 1579.

The *Golden Hind* was now alone for the rest of her voyage.

101, 29. **Santiago.** Santiago was inland. Here used for its port Valparaiso.

102, 5. **botija.** An earthen jug or jar.

16. **presently.** At the present, immediately.

103, 1. **pesos.** A Spanish word for weight.

Valdivia. "And a great cross of gold, beset with emeralds, on which was nailed a god of the same metal." F. D.

2. **ducat.** A gold coin worth about 9*s*.

7. **piece.** See note p. 90, l. 24.

11. **trust them.** The next day, Dec. 20, they entered a harbour to the north of Coquimbo, and remained here for a month (until Jan. 19, 1579), repairing their ship and building a pinnace. Drake sailed southwards in the pinnace to look for his lost ships, but after one day's sailing, was driven back by the wind.

12. **Tarapaca.** On the coast of Chile, 20° 12′ S. Lat., now called Iquique, the port of Tarapaca, which is inland.

24. **Arica.** "This is the port where they discharge their merchandise that pass from Lima to Potosi, and to all other cities within the land; and likewise at this place they were wont to embark all the silver which they carried for Panama....Since Captain Drake was at this port they carry their silver by land to Lima, and lade no more treasure here, but only discharge the merchants' goods that come from Spain hither. Also they have built a fort at this place for the better safety of the inhabitants, and have planted it with ten pieces of ordnance, and every summer there lie in garrison a hundred soldiers besides the townsmen.

From hence he sailed to another port called Chuli. In which port was a ship that had three hundred thousand pesos of silver in bars, but they had sent horsemen from Arica to give advertisement of Drake's being on the coast, which news came but two hours to the town before his arrival at the said port."

(The people of Santiago had already sent messengers by land "to give warning unto them of Peru. How be it, by reason that the country between this place and Peru is not inhabited for the space of two hundred leagues, and many huge and cold mountains covered with snow lie in the way, the post was so long in performance of this journey that Captain Drake was upon the coast of Peru a month before the said post came thither: neither could they send any news by sea, because they were destitute of shipping.")

"Whereupon the master of the ship, having no leisure to carry his silver on shore, was forced to throw it into the sea in six fathom water, where his ship rode, and so to run on shore in the ship's boat. And Captain Drake coming aboard the ship was told by an Indian that the master had thrown the silver overboard. Wherefore, seeing that news began to run of him from town to town, he stayed not here, but ran along the coast...and coming to the harborough of Lima, called El Callao, being two leagues distant from Lima itself (for Lima standeth up into the land), he arrived there one day before the news of him was brought to Lima, and found the men in the ships without suspicion." From '*A Discourse of the West Indies and South Sea*, by Lopez Vaz, a Portuguese, which was intercepted with the author thereof, at the River of Plate by Captain Withrington and Captain Christopher Lister in the fleet set forth by the Right Honourable the Earl of Cumberland for the South Sea, in the year 1586.'

104, 3. Lima. Lima is inland. Its port (Callao) is meant.

14. **real.** A silver coin worth about 6*d*.

18. **Cacafuego.** "Spitfire."

23. **Payta.** In the north of Peru. The *Cacafuego* had fourteen days' start of them, but sailed slowly owing to her heavy weight of treasure. They caught her up "on St David's day, being the first of March."

105, 2. John Drake. Drake's young nephew.

11. **San Francisco.** In Ecuador, a little to the north of the Equator.

23. **Cacaplata.** "Spitplate." There was enough silver to ballast the *Golden Hind*. There is some confusion here. The name of the ship was *Our Lady of the Conception*, master and owner, San Juan de Anton. She carried neither artillery nor arms. *Cacafuego* was probably Drake's ship, and *Cacaplata* the Spanish.

106, 1. a Spanish gentleman. Don Francisco de Zarate. His vessel was seized by Drake on April 4, near Acajutla, off the coast of Guatemala. On April 16 he wrote a letter (still in existence) to the Viceroy of Mexico, which is full of most interesting details about Drake and his ship. See Introduction, note 1, p. xviii.

5. **Guatulco.** Or Aguatulco. In New Spain (i.e. Mexico), 16° N. Lat., 96° W. Long. It was the port where the Spanish merchants embarked their goods for Peru and Honduras. See note p. 107, l. 14.

107, 11. his Portugal pilot. Nuño da Silva. His account of Drake's voyage from the Cape Verde Islands to Guatulco is given by Hakluyt.

14. **Canno.** A small island (also called Island of Canoes) off the coast of Central America, about six miles from the mainland. There is an error in the narrative. They arrived at Canno about

the middle of March, remained there until the 24th, and did not reach Guatulco until April 13. There they stayed until April 26, letting Nuño da Silva go an hour or two before they sailed.

16. **discharged her.** Took the cargo out of her.

graved her. Cleaned the bottom.

32. **the Straits.** The Viceroy of Peru had sent three ships, with six hastily made cannon, and two hundred and fifty men after Drake. They arrived at Cape San Francisco three weeks after he had taken the so-called *Cacafuego*, and hearing that he had not gone to Panama, concluded that he would return by the Straits of Magellan, and sailed back to Lima. The Viceroy then sent two ships either to intercept Drake in the Straits, or to see whether they could be fortified to prevent foreign ships for the future from passing through.

According to F. D., Drake intended to discover and return by a passage round the north of America, but partly owing to the extreme cold which discouraged his men, and partly owing to contrary winds, he abandoned the idea and decided to run for the Moluccas.

108, 11. **Buena Esperanza.** Cape of Good Hope.

29. **good bay.** In California. If 38° is correct, the bay of San Francisco. F. D. gives 38° 30′: in which case it was a small bay north of the bay of San Francisco. (A bay about 25 miles north-west of San Francisco is now called Drake's Bay.) Here they remained for a month—from June 17 until July 23—and prepared the ship for her homeward voyage.

109, 8. **cauls.** Small caps.

17. **kemb.** Comb.

110, 28. **artificially.** Skilfully.

32. **stinted.** Even those that may wear them are not allowed to wear more than a certain number, according to their rank.

111, 2. **coney.** Rabbit. For a description of the animal, see p. 113.

113, 17. **a want.** A mole.

114, 5. **a piece of sixpence.** Elizabeth (1558–1603) issued a dated sixpence yearly for upwards of forty years.

9. **of the country.** They were mistaken in thinking that the Spaniards had not previously explored this part of the coast.

21. **glass.** Having a gloss.

24. **bravery.** For the sake of a handsome appearance.

115, 6. **Tagulada.** Tagulandang, north-west of Celebes.

9. **The 14 of November.** A mistake for " The 4 of November."

12. **Mutyr.** Motir.

24. **the Portugal.** "Who had the command of Tidore." F. D.

116, 20. **states.** Estates = men of property.

21. **cloth of Calicut.** Calico, named from the Indian trading port, from which it came originally.

117, 7. **calivers.** Large pistols.

8. **one full yard.** A small cast gun of about a yard in length.

33. **figo.** Plantain.

118, 21. **Romans.** F. D. explains this as meaning 'strangers.' **ligiers.** Resident agents.

32. **Cordovan skin.** Cordovan leather. A celebrated leather was made at Cordova, in Spain.

119, 24. **little island.** Here they pitched tents, and entrenched themselves for fear of being attacked. Then they landed the cargo, and set up a smith's forge, and burnt charcoal to supply it with fuel. "The place affording us not only all necessaries... but also wonderful refreshing to our wearied bodies by the comfortable relief and excellent provision that here we found, whereby of sickly, weak, and decayed (as many of us seemed to be before our coming hither), we in short space grew all of us to be strong, lusty, and healthful persons....This island we called Crab Island." F. D. They left it on Dec. 12, and beat up and down among the shoals and islands until Jan. 9, when they were nearly wrecked.

32. **fiery worms.** Fireflies.

120, 21. **1579.** 1580, according to our reckoning. Previous to 1752 the year legally began on March 25. According to this old method of reckoning the year 1579 would not end until March 24.

121, 10. **Barateve.** Batjan.

122, 13. **Java major.** This name for Java was derived from Marco Polo. They left Batjan on February 10, and passing many islands on the way reached Java on March 9, and left it on March 26.

23. **pintado.** Originally a kind of chintz made in India. Here a coloured garment.

124, 9. **one kind.** The mangrove tree. The seeds germinate upon the tree, sending down large roots, and forming a great network.

12. **third of November.** According to F. D. they arrived at Plymouth on the 26 of September, "which was Monday in the just and ordinary reckoning of those that had stayed at home in one place or country, but in our computation was the Lord's day or Sunday." John Drake in his examination before the Inquisition at Lima, in 1587, says: "On reaching Plymouth they enquired from some fishermen 'How was the Queen,' and learnt that 'She was in health, but that there was much pestilence in Plymouth.'

So they did not land, but Captain Drake's wife and the mayor of the port came to see him on the ship." Drake afterwards went by road to London with some of the gold and silver, and a month after arriving at Plymouth took his ship up the Thames, and unloaded the rest of the silver at the Tower. "The Queen said that they were to make a house wherein the ship could be preserved as a memorial. She named Captain Francis Sir Francis, which is the same as 'Don,' and received him well, showing him great honour. There was a day on which he conversed with the Queen nine times, and people said that no one had ever enjoyed such an honour." John Drake: Second Declaration. (From *New Light on Drake*.)

CAVENDISH. FIRST VOYAGE

126, 13. **furniture.** Armour, weapons, and other equipment and stores.

127, 2. **Rio del Oro.** River of Gold. From early times there was a report that a great river with golden sands flowed from central Africa into the Atlantic. The Portuguese explorers hoped that this bay was the mouth of the river.

5. **canters.** See p. 88, l. 15.

16. **put room.** Set our course.

128, 29. **Port of Portugal.** Oporto.

129, 25. **chirurgeons.** Surgeons. Probably barbers, who used to perform small surgical operations as well as their usual work.

130, 2. **buffes.** Buffaloes.

22. **use at.** Resort.

131, 15. **river of Janeiro.** Rio de Janeiro (River of January), so named by the Portuguese from the month in which they discovered it, and because they thought that the great harbour was the estuary of a river.

132, 7. **Port Desire.** After the name of his ship.

22. **cowl-staves.** Poles for carrying tubs or baskets which have two ears.

134, 2. **grave.** To clean a ship's bottom by burning off accretions, and tarring.

6. **forty score.** Forty score yards.

135, 2. **artificial.** See note p. 110, l. 28.

136, 6. **Straits of Magellan.** In consequence of Drake's voyage, the King of Spain decided to fortify a narrow part of the straits, and so prevent the passage of enemies for the future. (These

straits were then believed to be the only way into the Pacific, and
that Tierra del Fuego was part of an unknown Southern Continent.)
A small town was built at the mouth of the straits, and another
—King Philip's City—in the centre on the continental side. Four
hundred Spaniards—men and women—were left there.

23. piece. Gun.

137, 29. River of Plate. The estuary of La Plata.

138, 3. Cape Froward. The most southerly point of the
mainland.

140, 12. dilvered. Tired.

22. caliver. See note p. 117, l. 7.

141, 12. cades. Barrels.

142, 17. Bay of Quintero. 32° S. Lat. In Chile, to the
north of Valparaiso.

26. shot. Shooters. 'A gun' is now used for one of a shooting
party.

30. score. See note p. 134, l. 6.

146, 2. bidings. Abodes

147, 1. minion. A gun.

12. botijas. See note p. 102, l. 5.

148, 12. scaped. Escaped. This form is still used in scape-
goat and scapegrace.

24. St Iago. See note p. 101, l. 29.

149, 15. Pisca. In Peru, south of Callao. There is still a
Cape Paracas and a town Pisco.

151, 2. targets. Shields.

15. sixteen. Previously he says "eighteen," p. 150.

16. Guiaquil. Guayaquil, the chief port of Ecuador.

27. Cordovan skins. See note p. 118, l. 32.

28. manteca de puerco. Lard.

pintados. See note p. 122, l. 23.

152, 14. bloody ensign. A red flag.

28. reals. See note p. 104, l. 14.

153, 10. Puna. In the Gulf of Guayaquil.

24. botijas. See note p. 102, l. 5.

25. bash. Bast, a fibrous bark, especially of the lime-tree.

154, 3. shadow. A kind of sedan-chair.

16. balsa. A raft.

156, 17. cods. Pods.

23. pompions. Pumpkins.

158, 12. **snap-hance.** A gun with a spring lock.

159, 31. **Nueva España.** New Spain. The name was given to Mexico, but also included other parts of Central America. Here Costa Rica.

160, 17. **Sonsonate.** No longer in Guatemala, but in Salvador.

24. **Aguatulco.** Guatulco. See note, p. 106, l. 5.

31. **cacaos.** Seeds of a tropical tree, from which cocoa and chocolate are made.

anil. Indigo.

32. **burnt their town, with the church.** A large crucifix escaped destruction, and became famous in consequence. Its fragments are still considered miraculous.

161, 10. **flasket.** A long shallow basket. Sometimes also a washing-tub.

27. **Customer.** Collector of customs.

162, 14. **Nueva Galicia.** Part of Mexico, now Jalisco.

20. **St Iago.** Santiago, in the province of Jalisco.

164, 3. **Mazatlan.** In the province of Sinaloa, Mexico.

19. **scape.** See note p. 148, l. 12.

165, 8. **St Lucar.** Now Cape San Lucas, at the extreme south of the long peninsula of Lower California.

166, 11. **fights.** Canvas spread out in a sea-fight to conceal the men from the enemy.

167, 21. **pesos.** See page 103, ll. 1, 2.

168, 5. **garbanzos.** Chick-peas.

peason. An old plural for peas.

170, 3. **Guana.** Guam, the largest of the Marianne or Ladrone Islands, at the extreme south of the group.

171, 15. **artificially.** See note p. 110, l. 28.

28. **yare.** Quick. Cf. the opening of Shakespeare's *Tempest*: "Fall to't yarely, or we run ourselves aground: bestir, bestir."

30. **prevent.** Get in front of: anticipate. Cf. " Prevent us, O Lord, in all our doings."

32. **lying at hull.** Lying-to (with a small amount of canvas set). "To hull" sometimes also means to drive without sail, oar, or rudder.

Cf. "He look'd, and saw the Ark hull on the flood."

Milton, *Par. Lost* XI.

"I am to hull here a little longer."

Shakespeare, *Twelfth Night*, I. iv.

172, 13. Manilla. Now Luzon, Manila being its chief town, and capital and chief port of the Philippines.

23. Sanguelos. People from Sanga in Japan. Pretty recognizes the wonderful skill and artistic feeling of the Japanese craftsmen.

175, 4. the other ship. The *Content*, in which there had been signs of mutiny, did not follow them when they left the haven of Aguada Segura (near Cape San Lucas in California), and they never saw her again. The Spanish pilot supposed that she had gone to discover a passage homewards round the north of America.

176, 13. saker. A small cannon.

18. Manilla. See note p. 172, l. 13.

25. Panama. Panay, south-west of Masbate.

177, 4. weirs. Enclosures of stakes for trapping fish.

178, 16. steads. Places. Cf. instead, steadfast, etc.

26. as big as England. The island of Negros, south of Panay, is about 130 miles long.

179, 12. Gilolo, Batochina. In the north of the Moluccas.

30. falcon. A cannon of $2\frac{1}{2}$ inch bore, carrying a 2 lb shot.

180, 6. Java Minor and Java Major. Java Minor was Bali, the island immediately to the east of Java. Java Major (Java) was at one time believed to be the northern part of a continent, and this belief lingered even after Del Cano, Drake, and Cavendish had sailed past its southern coast. See also note p. 122, l. 13.

181, 7. tuliban. Turban.

182, 18. plates. Flat pieces.

183, 14. our queen. He was in exile at the court of Elizabeth.

184, 14. all-to. Entirely, completely.

bebathe. Bathe all over.

185, 8. Sangles. See note p. 172, l. 23.

23. Crosiers. The constellation of the Southern Cross.

188, 10, causey. Causeway.

12. pompions. See note p. 156, l. 23.

189, 27. score. See note, p. 134, l. 6.

190, 29. Calicut cloth. See note p. 116, l. 21.

192, 17. Spanish Fleet. The pursuit of the remnant of the Armada had ceased a fortnight before.

194, 14. use. See note, p. 130, l. 22.

LE MAIRE AND SCHOUTEN'S VOYAGE

196, 13. **we saw land on starboard.** The south-east corner of Tierra del Fuego, at the entrance of Le Maire Strait.

198, 6. **roads.** Roadsteads: anchorages.

8. **porpoises.** Probably *seals.*

21. **loefward.** Windward.

199, 25. **we called Cape Horn.** After Hoorn, the town in Holland, to which their ships belonged. One of these was also named the *Hoorn.*

201, 15. **it should rather have been called William Schouten's Strait.** Probably a suggestion of Schouten himself, who appears to have been jealous of Le Maire. He managed to get the first edition of the journal of the voyage published under his own name, but later editions were published under that of Le Maire.

www.ingramcontent.com/pod-product-compliance
Ingram Content Group UK Ltd.
Pitfield, Milton Keynes, MK11 3LW, UK
UKHW042142280225
455719UK00001B/44